THE ROOT OF ALL HEALING

Seven Steps to Healing Anything

Seven Steps to Healing Anything

Misa Hopkins

iUniverse, Inc.

New York   Bloomington

The Root of All Healing
7 Steps to Healing Anything

iUniverse books may be ordered through booksellers or by contacting:

iUniverse
1663 Liberty Drive
Bloomington, IN 47403
www.iuniverse.com
1-800-Authors (1-800-288-4677)

ISBN: 978-1-4401-3923-9 (pbk)
ISBN: 978-1-4401-3924-6 (ebk)

Printed in the United States of America

iUniverse rev. date: 5/14/2009

For more information:
www.misahopkins.com

To you—

the courageous individuals

who embrace healing as

a journey to freedom.

_____

There are only two ways to live your life.

One is as though nothing is a miracle.

The other is as though everything is a miracle.

—Albert Einstein

Contents

Disclaimer

Let me be very clear that the opinions in this book are just that—my opinions based upon years of observing, recording and studying the nature of healing as a spiritual journey. It is a shame that in order to offer personal opinions and observations about healing, I need to make a disclaimer for the protection of my person, family, publisher and profession that I am not a medical expert and I am not dispensing medical advice. Later in this book you will read my views about how our society's habit of refusing to take responsibility for our own lives is creating greater harm than good in our ethical development and the progress of individual healing. That said, if you use any information in this book without the advice of a licensed medical doctor or licensed psychologist or psychiatrist, you do so at your own risk, with a willingness to assume full responsibility for your own physical, mental and emotional well-being, which is ultimately a more fulfilling way to live life.

Preface—How This Book Can Help You

If you are reading this book, you have probably tried more than one healing methodology, yet are experiencing minimal to no progress in your healing. There are reasons many of us continue to suffer through illness and *The Root of All Healing* will reveal some of the reasons people don't heal, as well as offer simple yet significant insights that can help you experience true and lasting healing.

Many of us have accepted the conventional practice of giving up our personal power and leaving it to the "experts." This conventional wisdom is based on an old model, dating back to the 1600's, of treating the body more like a machine or an object that needed to be completely understood and controlled. It became an accepted belief that only people with certain educational expertise were able to repair the body when it became ill or injured. Though the intentions of any given expert may be notable, their skills extensive, and their ability to help us heal profound, this surrendering of power often leaves us feeling completely helpless to the will of our bodies and the current knowledge and theories of others. It has been my observation such feelings of powerlessness can keep us remaining ill until we discover the hidden powers of self-healing within us.

While the body may indeed be the physical vehicle of the human journey, and a vehicle better treated as it is better understood, the journey of the human is about the evolution of the spirit as much as it is about the functions of the body. Without spirit our progress is limited, for it is human spirit that overcomes the greatest challenges, drives us to discover greater knowledge, and sustains us in hope. It is the human spirit that beats the odds and continually redefines the playing field of human existence.

The foundation of *The Root of All Healing* is about claiming our personal power and recognizing our healing as a Divine journey that each of us embarks upon through our bodies, minds, emotions and spirits in our own unique ways. The healing journey gives us an opportunity, through our ineffable spirits, to discover our personal power—the living, breathing reality of our own creative and Divine nature.

When I say spiritual or Divine, I am not talking about religion. Religion is not a necessary ingredient for healing—not even faith healing. If that were true, I would have been dead many years ago, along with many of my closest friends and colleagues. While I hold a deep respect for religions, I consider myself as a spiritual person rather than a religious one. When I speak about the spiritual or Divine, I am talking about a power within life that flows through all of us that we can access in our personal journeys of healing. How you define that power for yourself is entirely up to you.

I urge you to read this book from beginning to end. I tend to be one of those people who like to flip open to pages anywhere in the book and read for a while. This would *not* be the best way to read this book. My first career was as a teacher, and so this book is written with new concepts building upon previous ones. You will get the most out of it by reading one consecutive page at a time. I know this is contrary to our "sound bite" oriented world, but claiming one's power in healing is more like a seven course meal than a fast-food fix.

If you were inspired to pick up this book, then you are someone who is probably very dedicated to your well-being and I commend your dedication, even if you may be feeling discouraged, frustrated, or stuck at the moment. I understand those feelings very well, so know from the beginning I fully empathize with you. Because I can't stand to be stuck, I had to discover hope. I had to discover the profound healing power within me. Because I didn't have a lot of money to put into professional assistance, I had to find the well of healing wisdom living within my subconscious and apply it with conviction for my own well-being. In truth, it would have been easier to linger in despair. So if you are reading this book, I trust you are someone who is willing to engage your will and creativity to becoming healed. My deepest desire is that in reading this book, you will find the source of your own hope—and more importantly, a deeper commitment to your own power to heal.

Acknowledgements

Writing a book has been a humbling experience for me. With each insight I shared, I was very much aware that what I have learned, I learned most often with the help of someone else. Courageous individuals in their paths of healing have taught me what it means to be optimistic, persevere, have faith, feel compassion, observe life on many levels, welcome truth, and most of all—use the process of healing to open a doorway to Divine awareness and spiritual freedom. I am grateful to each and every teacher in my life, from the children with serious illnesses I met as an in-home instructor, to the energy healers who opened me to greater states of Divine grace, to the people who allowed me to sing them their death songs as they completed their journeys by transitioning to the other side. Each person helped me see the sacred moments in every healing journey as epiphanies of awareness in Divine consciousness.

My mother is the one who helped me see the precious gift of healing energy that lived inside of me, and I am especially grateful for her influence in my personal journey with healing sounds. I am equally grateful to my father, who called to me from the spirit world, inviting me to sing to him as he made his way to the other side through death—the ultimate surrender to God. Because of the suffering they endured before they died, my commitment to living as free from suffering as possible, and helping others who choose the same path, led me to writing this book. Witnessing their suffering and experiencing my own has been powerful motivation to experience healing freedom. I am grateful for every event that has catapulted me into seeking and finding the sacred—the source of true spiritual freedom—within healing.

I awoke with the title of the book on the tip of my tongue three mornings in a row, not knowing it was a book until I finally wrote the words, "The Root of All Healing" on a piece of paper, and just kept on writing. It seems to me the Divine consciousness flowing through me early in the morning chose a great title. I'm grateful for such a meaningful name and the inspiration that came with it.

Several friends helped me sort through appropriate subtitles and I appreciate the thoughtful suggestions each person gave. My dear friend, Ariann Thomas spent countless hours listening to me discuss various aspects of the book and provided me with meaningful feedback. She, Marci Mongelli and my husband, Jeffrey Burger, all proofed the book and made sure the concepts presented were clear. My editor, Laurel Stuart's insights were most valuable. Friends who had self-published and marketed their own books were generous with time and information as I struggled with decisions about how to get this book out into the world. Krystalya Marié, Chris Davis, Barney Davey and Egan Sanders all contributed to its physical birth. Lisa Diaz and Cheryl McDaniel offered wonderful creative ideas for the development of the website so that I would have an inspiring place to connect with readers and other individuals on their healing journeys.

Participants in my classes, knowingly or not, have challenged me to go deeper into my own healing journey, stretching beyond my perceived limits at any given time, so that I could share my own stories of hope and conscious miracle making with them. In my desire to inspire them and in witnessing their own healing successes, I became inspired myself. As a result I have experienced personal healing miracles that might not otherwise have occurred.

In my dreams and in the physical, I have met some of the most extraordinary guides and teachers. My life has certainly been proof that when the student is ready the teacher will come, because I have rarely sought out a teacher. They are too numerous to mention here, but I hold each one of them in my heart with deep respect and admiration.

Two friends and elders, Harvest Moon and Ariann Thomas, have for several years been observing me as I make my choices on my life path, holding me accountable to walk in this world with love and integrity. I hope that anyone who is serious about serving others is as fortunate as I am to have found individuals both loving and truthful to help me stay clear from the trappings of my own ego.

And then there is my cherished husband. I am so fortunate to be married to Jeffrey Burger, who offered emotional, physical, and financial support to me so that I could write this book. Because my most inspired time for writing occurs at about the same time we would normally be preparing dinner, Jeffrey did a lot of the cooking at our house. On top of that, he offered many significant suggestions that improved the book and some great ideas for branding and marketing. He believed in the importance of making this book available, and because of him, you are able to read it now.

Introduction—Where The Healing Begins

In 1994, I received a call from my brother telling me my mother was in the hospital and not expected to live through the week. I had not spoken to my mother in years because I had chosen to take some time away from her in order to do some deep emotional healing around our relationship. My brother and I sensed she wanted some closure before she crossed over, so I made the decision to go to her quickly. While making the trip home, I reassured myself I would create emotional safety and understanding with my mother so that I could continue my life, and she could cross over with love and resolution between us. We had not seen each other for two years, and from the perspective of some, I was the prodigal daughter returning home. From my perspective, I had finally completed enough of my personal physical and emotional healing to be able to hold space for the emotional pain she was in and had been in most of her life.

When I arrived at the hospital in the late afternoon, I was told a nurse had given her an extra dose of morphine because family and staff were concerned about how Mom would react to me coming home. Deep inside I knew Mom would be just fine. Because I no longer carried anger and resentment toward my mother, I was confident I could stand calmly in my center with whatever feelings she might be having at this time. By holding both of us in this sacred way, I knew I could help her access her own truth and finally experience some deep emotional tranquility. Knowing my mother, I was certain she would want to make peace with me before releasing herself from this physical world, and I was ready to help her find her freedom.

Taking a deep, centering breath, I walked into her room, over to her bedside, and reached for her hand. I told her I had resolved the painful memories of my childhood and that everything was all right. She looked deep into my eyes, like a child hoping to find acceptance, asking for my forgiveness. Finally she found the words to tell me she was sorry and assured me she loved me. I didn't tell her I forgave her. I told her I understood. After years of inner healing work, I knew real forgiveness comes when the resentments are gone and in its place we truly understand the source of our own pain and the pain of others.

We talked a while with a depth of regard and concern I had never experienced before that day. As the sun fell behind the hills, my mother grew quieter as the morphine finally demanded she sleep. Without even thinking, I started humming to her, the same way I hummed my brothers and sister to sleep when I was a child. A beautiful Native American chant, unknown to me until that moment, spontaneously welled up from my heart and as my mother listened she wept, perhaps her own Native blood stirred by the music.

The doctors didn't know what was wrong with my mother. She was too weak for exploratory surgery so they put her on a penicillin drip for any possible infection along with some morphine for the pain, and given her condition, recommended the family be called. After singing my song, and without any warning, I discovered the source of her current physical pain. I could suddenly see inside her body where I observed what I would describe as a bronchial infection. I could see nothing wrong with her heart, which was a major source of concern to her doctor. Silently, I asked her spirit what she needed. I then saw a beautiful and bright emerald green light fill the places inside her where I had seen the infection. I watched in quiet awe as the green transformed into white and the vision disappeared.

By this time the sun was completely behind the hill and my sister, as if on cue, walked into the darkening room. Enveloped in the hallowed moment of day becoming night, she sat down next to my mother. I was already holding one of Mom's hands. She picked up the other and reached for my empty hand. There the three women of our family sat in the silence and the darkness—for the first time ever, being together without words.

About an hour later, my dad, brothers, nieces and nephews found their way to Mom's room. Instead of lying weakly on the bed like a woman who was getting ready to die, my mother was sitting up in bed laughing with the rest of her rowdy family, cheeks full of color and beaming. When the doctor came in to check on her, he looked puzzled as Mom asked him when she could go home. He had to agree she was looking much better, held her a day for observation and sent her home, assuming the penicillin drip had helped her. She stayed with us here on earth for another three months before finally making her journey to the other side.

I received a profound gift from my mother before she left this earth. After witnessing the power of love, sound, and intention heal my mother, I launched myself into an even deeper journey of my own emotional and physical healing, eventually evolving into opportunities to help others as well. Since that day, sometimes on my own and sometimes with the help of competent physicians, alternative healers, and my own energy medicine I have healed myself from a life-threatening hormone imbalance, and a collapsing ovary and fallopian tube. I completely sealed up a cut, normally requiring stitches, within less than 24 hours using sound and intention. I have stopped colds with nothing more than sound and symbols, healed infections with light and sound, and freed myself from limitations of multiple sclerosis using my own sound medicine.

I have been privileged to support people in their healing journeys as together we healed a weak heart by growing a new heart valve, sealed an intestinal rupture that had caused intestinal fluid to seep out into the body, stabilized the activity of red and white blood cells, eliminated cancerous tumors and more. I find these moments to be wonderful reminders about our healing potential as humans. Each time profound healing occurs for someone I am able to help or for me, I am humbled as I witness our tremendous capacity to re-create ourselves over and over into healthier, more vital beings.

I am equally touched by the power of the human spirit. In my first career, as a Special Education teacher, I spent one year teaching terminally ill children in their homes. Over time some of the children made their transition to the other side, but before they left each one of them made an imprint on the hearts of many of us who were privileged to know them. Though their bodies grew weaker, their spirits soared, resilient and strong in their loving regard and compassion for others. They taught me that healing is a journey, sometimes resulting in great physical achievement as they frequently brought themselves back from the brink of death and sometimes resulting in the great spiritual awareness that occurs when we cross over.

Those I have known who have embraced their healing journey have further shown me that the true power and measure of our existence here on earth is in how we live out our lives. Because illness insists we pay attention to how we are living, healing becomes an opportunity to look at what truly gives meaning to our lives. As we determine what is truly important to us, we discover the essence of who we are. This may be the single greatest gift the healing journey gives to us.

A year or so before my father died, I asked him what he perceived to be the mission of his life. He bowed his head thoughtfully, then looked intently into my eyes and said, "I'm here to suffer for the people." My father was a deeply spiritual man, so when I asked him to explain it was no surprise to hear him tell me he willingly accepted suffering so that others would not have to. For him, this was a form of prayer. Both of my parents died from cancer. Indeed they both suffered greatly before they made their journey to the other side of the veil. At least I have the comfort of knowing my father accepted suffering willingly, finding personal strength by offering it up for the well-being of others. I also realize he may have chosen suffering that was never necessary for him to endure. However, because of his willingness to share his mission with me, I learned something important about healing from my father.

When illness grabs hold of me and I am suffering, I remind myself that my father and other compassionate people who have gone before him have offered prayers that their suffering be the last suffering. Then I ask myself if I am willing to receive the gift of their prayers. I ask myself if I am willing to let go of the suffering, and devote my strength to finding my relief and complete wellness. Sometimes relief comes quickly. Sometimes it comes after much effort. And if relief is slow in coming, like my father, I offer up my suffering as a prayer that perhaps someone in greater pain than me will find relief in this moment.

Because of my mother and father's influence, and their painful deaths, I am devoted to healing myself and supporting others in finding freedom from pain. I am delighted when I can offer healing support and relief from pain to my client or when I release myself from physical and emotional pain. I am greatly pleased when I can maintain for myself and help others maintain vigorous health and well-being through thoughtful daily practices. I have become committed to the concept of creating life physically free and happy, and that is the life I live today.

Healing is a journey, so what I have to share in this book is what I have discovered along the way. Some of the discoveries I share may seem unbelievable, others may seem extremely obvious, and when it comes to healing I find it is the obvious that often eludes us. Though I have been actively involved in natural healing for over 15 years, I am constantly in awe of how the simplest treatment, or the slightest change of perception or behavior (that in retrospect seems obvious) can make a vast difference in my health. As this awareness has become increasingly apparent, I have made a commitment to break through my preconceived perceptions about what needs to be healed and how healing is supposed to occur, allowing a greater mystery to unfold itself in my body as I witness how healing truly can be. Because I now allow myself to enter fully into the mystery of healing, without so many preconceived concepts or sole reliance on conventional treatments, seeming miraculous occurrences become normal occurrences. I look at some of these "miraculous" healings with the realization I have witnessed only the surface of the potential that lives within us all.

Some of my own real-life stories I debated sharing because for some they will seem too fantastic. For me, they were simply a part of my journey. Some of these healing stories are moments where the mystery unveiled itself and I experienced what I knew to be ancient, and yet for me, new ways of gentle healing. I include them because they speak to the great healing potential I believe lives inside every one of us. During the moments I touch that potential, I am inspired to continue on in my day-to-day journey, and it is my hope these stories will inspire others as well in their own unique healing journeys.

Whenever I am helping someone, I am very clear the healing journey is theirs, not mine. More than once I have had someone come to me looking for a miracle cure. They are tired of being sick and want to get on with fulfilling their life purpose, or at least more meaningful work. This is certainly understandable. There have been many times, in my own journey, I desperately wished someone would take out a magic wand and cure me. I had so many goals I would have been accomplishing if I just felt better. It is very difficult to even think about creating prosperity, engaging in a new career, or attracting the love of your life when you don't feel well. I'm not at all surprised when someone comes looking to me for a fast answer.

Yet, whenever someone thinks they need me in order to heal and they are not active participants in their own healing, I know we won't get very far. As I have said before, healing is a personal journey. I can help and that is all. The true healing happens between the person choosing to be healed and his or her own relationship with the Divine power that dwells within them. The healing journey is each person's opportunity to discover the life-giving, creative force of the Divine living within their own consciousness, and so I can be of assistance, but I certainly can't do it for someone.

Sometimes we do indeed witness what appear to be instant healings. In my experience, this happens when someone is in a very receptive space with heart and mind fully ready to receive complete healing. More often; however, healing is a process of time, where the person is releasing old, stuck patterns that keep them feeling ill and replacing those patterns with healthier beliefs and habits. Or the person is teaching their body over time to respond in a different manner to an agent inside their body that has been wreaking havoc. Even with seemingly instant healings, the person who is healed will then need to fully embrace the new behavior or belief that allowed full healing to occur, and weave this new awareness into daily consciousness.

Healing is a practice of dedication and self-love, because very often getting to the root cause—the source of the—condition is necessary for full and complete recovery. New belief systems and patterns of behavior need to be deeply anchored in both the subconscious and conscious mind if healing transformation is going to last. Especially in the cases of chronic illness and depression, making sure both the physical and emotional bodies are addressed is imperative if the healed person wants to prevent recurrences.

Even if a medical practitioner is adequately helping me treat the source of my physical discomfort, I know after years of self-healing work, there is a strong likelihood I will find an emotional root behind or accompanying the physical pain. I make sure I treat the physical and emotional roots, or the emotional effects, of the illness. I don't tend to see much separation any more between physical and emotional pain, because I know before I experience complete well-being, I need to heal on every level. For example, when I had been exposed to environmental toxins, I knew I needed to respond to my emotional feelings about having been affected by something in my environment I didn't put there. And when my hormones were extremely out of balance (I was an adult woman producing as much testosterone as a boy in puberty.), I knew I needed to understand and heal the psychological reason my female body was becoming male, seemingly on its own and without my conscious permission.

To understand my abnormal hormone production, I began listening to urgings from my silent meditations to embrace yet more stillness and less activity in my life. In a process of getting quiet and listening with compassion to my thoughts and feelings, I uncovered and healed the abuse that caused me to break faith with being feminine. Along with talk therapy, well-prescribed hormone therapy, some deep emotional processing, and the support of skilled healers from several healing disciplines, I finally brought my body and emotions into balance.

I have found the same to be true for my clients. Those who address the emotional content behind or accompanying the physical illness tend to heal more rapidly and with more lasting results. When someone tells me no physical treatment they have tried is making any long-term difference, I recommend they consult their emotions. Buried feelings of emotional pain are often blocking even the most aggressive healing treatments, or they can even cause resistance in identifying and fully receiving the best treatment for our condition. More than once, I have recommended my client enter into therapy with a psychologist so they can understand their emotions, experience self-compassion, and ultimately heal by developing stabilizing perspectives that calm the influence of overwhelming emotions.

Every now and then, a new client tells me I couldn't possibly understand how difficult the journey has been for them because my life is so easy. Their observation is understandable, because I do live a fairly effortless and very fulfilling life—now. However, in the past, my own emotional or physical pain has been so intense, I entertained thoughts of suicide, so I know how daunting the healing journey can be. At one point, after years of a constant roller coaster ride with my health and emotions, I finally said to myself, "Stop dancing on the edge. Make a choice. Do you want to live or die?" "And self," I said, "don't answer until you know which decision you are willing to accept with complete and full responsibility for the outcome."

Obviously, I chose to live and with that choice, I consciously made a commitment to discover how to live a happy, healthy life. I told myself I would not accept constant or chronic illness, or depression as a way of living. I would do whatever it took to live the life I wanted to live. That commitment eventually led me to a journey of significant self-healing and with it came momentous personal growth. There were many times I didn't know how to create the happiness and wellness I desired on my own. At those times I sought help, and was blessed to find some wonderful healers from various disciplines. Like the people who sometimes come to me, I frequently wished one of the healers would take away my pain. As often as I yearned for an outside fix, there was a friend or therapist in my life reminding me that while it was good to receive help—the comfort, love, reassurances, worthiness, relief from my agony, and ultimately the creation of a self-loving life of health and happiness was truly within me—if I was willing to access that power.

In my case, as it has been for many of my clients, I needed help because I had been ill for so long I barely remembered what wellness felt like. When I got relief from my physical or emotional pain even for minutes, I could remember how wellness and happiness felt. I benefited from having someone assist me so that I could remember and hold those feelings in my awareness. Fortunately, my healers coached me to reinforce and affirm those feeling of health and happiness. As I reinforced the feelings I wanted to be experiencing, eventually, the painful, hurtful feelings were replaced with calm, peace and physical freedom.

Although now I do the vast majority of my personal healing work on my own, when I do seek medical assistance or alternative healing, I remain clear that I am the master of my body. Receiving aid whether holistic or conventional is a means of intelligently promoting my wellness, and my health is my job—not anyone else's. I do not treat the symptoms and assume the problem is gone. I use natural remedies, energy, prayers, and knowledgeable advice, and an occasional over-the-counter medicine to reinforce my internal commitment to health, until my commitment becomes my daily reality without the help of remedies and assistance. This intensity of commitment has been the catalyst not only for creating health, but more importantly, for developing a profound relationship with the Divine power within me.

Someone once said to me, "All paths lead to the Divine." When it comes to embracing my healing journey, those words became truth in action. Discovering the power of the Divine nature living inside me was and still is the greatest gift of the healing process. Learning how to heal myself from one ailment after another became paths or classrooms for understanding the ability of Divine creation that lived within me. Gradually, as the need for physical healing has decreased, I have been able to apply the same basic steps used in creating healing for creating greater happiness and fulfillment.

The human being's ability to heal is extraordinary. The power of love and intention a person can generate for healing is remarkable. Using the power of your mind and heart is in complete alignment with the laws of nature. Bodies regenerate themselves naturally. Sometimes we need to help our bodies remember how to do that healthily and if we choose to do this consciously, we embark on a healing journey.

I have discovered that when I invite healing in absolute clarity and love, my cells respond to their master—me. In that moment I am giving voice to the will of the Divine as it flows through me, and I have witnessed others discover this source of the Divine within themselves. The healing journey gives us the opportunity to discover this essence in profound and mysterious ways, with each experience being as unique as the individual who embarks on the journey. Exactly how you or I believe or experience the Divine is not important. However, in order to heal at your core it is important to know there is a power, energy, or source flowing through all of life including you, and you have the ability to access that source whenever you wish. You may give this source whatever name speaks to your soul. I call it the Divine.

For those of you reading this book who may be standing very close to your transition to the other side, I see merging with the Divine in such completeness as the goal of the spiritual and healing journey. Sometimes, the greatest act of healing is to surrender to the call to return home. More than once I have sung someone's sacred song as they died to this body and their souls entered the Divine light. I have seen and felt how splendid this act of ultimate surrender and gift of freedom can be. You may find the steps in this book serve you in your journey of surrender as well as someone who is going to be staying on this planet a while longer, because ultimately the healing journey is about a deeper awareness of the Divine presence within you.

As you read these seven healing steps, perhaps you will allow my reflections to stimulate your own thoughts and feelings about healing. This book simply offers guidelines—suggestions—born from years of observing the overall journey. However, the journey that counts for you is your own journey. May this book support you in accessing the root of your own healing, the Divine within you, so that you may experience a healthier, happier, more fulfilling existence.

In my heart and songs,
Reverend Misa

CHAPTER ONE — STEP ONE
DISCOVER THE HIDDEN STORIES BEHIND YOUR ILLNESS AND HEALTH

To understand the true cause of your illness, you must become an astute observer of your life, and you must do the same to discover your cure.

How often do you slow down and take a good look at your life? It is so easy to get caught up in the day-to-day functions of living; actually pausing to reflect on your life may seem like a nice, but unnecessary luxury. Yet, when it comes to healing, this is an important and necessary first step to claiming your well-being. Until you take the time to stop and observe, you are simply repeating the same old behaviors with the same old beliefs, and probably making very little progress. When you pause, observe and reflect, you begin receiving insights into how and why your illness exists, what is keeping you ill, and what you can do to become healthy.

BEHAVIORAL OBSERVATION

A couple of years ago, my digestion was terrible. Every time I ate, I felt like I was going to vomit as soon as I had finished eating. It seemed to take an entire day or two to digest the small amount of food I was eating. My husband and I eat primarily organic, non-processed food, so I couldn't figure out why I was having such a dramatic reaction. When I told my naturopathic physician about my condition, she suggested I

1

chart my intake of food and note how I was feeling immediately after eating and during the time between meals.

From the data I collected, my doctor was able to see how my diet was affecting my energy level. She recommended an entirely new diet prescribed for my blood type that would eliminate allergic reactions to food my body wasn't processing well. She sent me home to chart my diet and energy levels once again. Within a day of strictly adhering to my new diet, my digestion was dramatically improved. I was actually digesting my food immediately and feeling great. With a week of charting, I was able to see a direct correlation between the new diet and a greatly enhanced energy level. Through observation, I was able to understand, along with my doctor, my physical response to my former diet and recognize the benefits of making behavioral changes.

Because my doctor was wise enough to engage me in the discovery process, I learned to pay attention to what I was eating. Through my own observations, I discovered direct correlations between what I ate and how I felt. I was at least already aware of the unhealthy additives, chemicals and processing techniques used by a majority of food manufacturers (manufactured food—the words alone give a clue); and therefore, avoided many *so-called* foods because I knew they were more chemical than nutrition. I didn't have to eat them any more to know I experienced adverse effects. However, through this process of observation, I learned even many natural, organic foods were still not good for my particular body. Through my daily record keeping, I used my observational skills to notice what did and did not work for me. Although I don't maintain written records any longer, I continue to observe the effects of the food I eat today. By paying attention to how my body responds, I can better choose foods that actually nourish my particular body, thus providing me with greater health and vitality.

My husband recently discovered this in regard to his snoring. Because his snoring tends to wake me up, he had been looking for solutions to reduce or eliminate his tendency to occasionally snore. We were aware that snoring is normally considered to be a physiological event, but given my husband's snoring patterns I had a strong suspicion his snoring might be primarily psychological. Since he did not snore every night—only occasionally, I started to pay attention to what was going on during the day, prior to the nights he actually snored.

In my first career, as a Special Education teacher, I learned to record and interpret behavioral data. By recording what preceded any given behavior, the behavior itself, and the consequence—what followed the behavior, I was able to see patterns that triggered and reinforced a given behavior. In my observations of my husband's snoring, it appeared he seemed to snore on nights when he worked very late or had a lot on his mind. I shared this observation with him so he could determine what he wanted to do.

Months later, on one of our morning walks, he looked over at me and said, "Honey, do you realize I haven't snored, at least not enough to wake you, for over a week now?"

He was right. He hadn't been snoring, at least not loud enough to be noticeable.

"What do you think has changed?" I asked him.

"I stopped snoring when I hired a consultant to do some of the research on my project," he reflected.

"Why do you think that made a difference?" I asked him further.

"I trust him and he knows what he is doing. I think I'm just not worrying as much," he replied.

It would have been so much easier to assume snoring was simply a physiological condition with no cure other than surgery and left it at that. However, by observing what was happening before the snoring occurred, we were able to hypothesize it might be a psychological response, and therefore, there might be a way to curb his snoring behavior. When he joined me in the process of observing, he was able to notice his snoring decreased or stopped when his stress level was reduced. By observing what preceded the behavior—in this case, going from great anxiety to minimal anxiety during the day—he saw how his snoring behavior changed in response.

As mentioned earlier, sometimes the consequence, or what happens after the behavior, is a key in recognizing behavioral patterns. By observing the consequence, you can see how you are reinforcing certain behaviors in your life, either subconsciously or consciously. I spent a few days with a friend of mine who was challenged with chronic pain. While I was there, I noticed whenever she had a particularly bad day, she would go over to her cupboard, pull out a piece of chocolate and pop it in her mouth. This made complete sense to me. When you are having a difficult day, it is natural to want to make the day a little sweeter. However, because she was doing this on a regular basis, here is the message she was sending to herself. When I'm feeling bad I get chocolate. Feeling bad is the behavior. Getting chocolate is the consequence, and in this case, the chocolate became a reward that was probably reinforcing feeling bad. The better time to eat chocolate, if she wanted to encourage her body to feel better, was when she was feeling exceptionally well.

I can also create an undesirable outcome by denying or attempting to ignore the effects of the behavior. Here is something I might say to myself if I am denying the effects of a food that isn't good for me: "I know this isn't good for me, but I like it, so I'm going to eat it anyway." I've done this on more than one occasion with wheat, which my body is allergic to, and then paid the price for my decision. Later on with a constricted throat and very slow digestion, I am wondering why I didn't listen to my inner alarm bells going off before I took the bite. There is a reason I stubbornly refused to adhere to my own intelligent warning. I was getting something out of it I wanted in that moment, and so I decided it was worth the price.

This is often true with anything we are indulging including alcohol, caffeine, cigarettes, drugs, diets, sex, relationships and jobs. We indulge because we are getting something out of it. We are getting a desire or need fulfilled at some level, though we are meeting the need through an unhealthy means. We can become fulfilled through healthier means if we stop long enough to consider what need is being met and then further consider how we could meet it through a more beneficial means.

For example, the reason I eat wheat even though I know my body will react is my desire to be completely and fully in control of my body. I don't like the thought that my body doesn't like wheat because it puts limits on what I can eat. I have investigated to see if a traumatic event was associated with eating wheat, in order to psychologically shift my reaction, but found nothing. If my reaction to wheat was life threatening or severely distressing, I probably wouldn't risk even small amounts. But my physical reaction is discomfort that lasts for an hour or two—not enough to stop me. So in my desire to be in control I eat the wheat telling myself my mind is in charge, not my body—but the cells in my body haven't fully registered that yet, and I become ill. My body is telling me clearly it doesn't hold the same belief.

I love to eat out, and eliminating wheat completely can make food choices in restaurants extremely limiting. As I see it, the need I am fulfilling by eating something I'm allergic to is my ego desire to be fully in control of my body without any exceptions. So the first thing I need to do is to admit my ego is threatened. Further, I need to recognize the positive aspect of my ego that desires to create my own reality, while honoring my body (instead of ignoring it), which is clearly telling me wheat is not working. By choosing to honor my body, I can now focus on maintaining my health, rather than challenging it, and *involve my ego in protecting* my health. For the most part, I protect my health by not eating wheat. If I decide I want to eat something wheat-based, and I'm not sure about whether the wheat is organic (which I digest better than processed wheat), I eat a very small amount and observe how my body is handling it. Sometimes I can eat a little organically grown wheat without a reaction. I can rarely eat processed wheat without my throat swelling up. So, while my mind wants my body to be ok with eating any wheat, my body knows what is truly good for me when I stop and observe.

Following my agreement to eat only a little and then observe, I made a delightful discovery when my husband and I were on a French island in the Caribbean. I found I had very little reaction to any wheat I ate there, but continue to react to wheat here in the States. By observing, I can hypothesize that my allergic reaction is clearly not psychological, but very likely a physiological response to the difference between how wheat is generally grown and/or processed in the U.S. compared to another country. By observing carefully the relationship between the behavior—eating wheat and the consequence—my body's reaction, I have learned a great deal about how to keep myself feeling healthy and vital.

Consequences can also be punishments or be like punishments that limit a behavior. I have a friend who cannot drink red wine, not because she is an alcoholic, but because she gets blazing headaches whenever she drinks even the smallest amount. In this case, the reaction she gets from drinking the wine is like a punishment so severe, she refuses to drink it at all. If that were my reaction to wheat, it would be a severe enough reaction to keep me from ever putting a bite of it in my mouth.

LISTENING FOR THE CAUSE AS WELL AS THE CURE

Many of us have accepted the conventional practice of recognizing the symptoms and then looking for the cure. The problem with treating symptoms is that if you haven't treated the cause, the condition is likely to either recur or worsen. I know from personal experience that treating symptoms was of very little benefit to me.

As I shared earlier, many years ago, I suffered from a significant hormone imbalance. I had gone to multiple doctors for several years looking for someone who could offer me treatment that would make a difference. At the time, I didn't know I had a hormone imbalance. I only knew the symptoms I was experiencing. In rushed appointments, doctor after doctor would ask me to describe my symptoms. I always did my best, but the truth was I rarely remembered everything. In fact my general state of discomfort was pretty normal, so I was probably having symptoms it never occurred to me to mention. Each doctor, with good intentions and genuine concern, prescribed usually either estrogen or progesterone, which they believed might alleviate my symptoms and bring my body into greater hormonal balance. The hormones worked for a while, but overall, my condition grew worse every year. Treating the symptoms in hope that it would additionally address enough of the cause was never adequate.

Finally, a lovely friend suggested I visit an endocrinologist she highly recommended. When she told me about some of his successes with women having more severe symptoms than mine, I scheduled a visit. In the mail, his clinic staff sent me some paperwork to fill out, including a request for a description of my symptoms. The checklist they provided listed symptoms I had never even thought about. I dutifully checked everything that applied and then read the general instructions at the end, which read something like, "List every symptom you can think of whether or not you think it applies." I must have spent a half-hour writing out symptoms. I would think I was finished, only to go back to add another one.

When I arrived at the appointment, I was told to take my list with me into the exam room. A doctor with a warm smile greeted me, read my list and then said, "Now, tell me about your symptoms." I was surprised. He had just read my lengthy list, but still wanted me to tell him what was happening with me, so I told him everything that was already on my list, plus some other symptoms that came to mind. When I finished, he asked if there was anything more. I did not feel rushed or hurried. I felt as though he was going to sit there with me until I squeezed out every bit of information that was inside me. When I finished, he asked me several more questions for clarification. Then he told me he was going to run a series of tests to confirm his theory, and explained to me very carefully the chemical interactions that were probably going on in my body creating the specific series of symptoms I was experiencing. He ran the tests and his assessment confirmed I was producing as much testosterone as a boy in puberty. He assured me it would take many years of treatment to teach my hormones how to function properly and that it could be done. He used the symptoms to understand the cause and then treated the cause directly.

When I got back in my car to drive home, I started crying. Touched to my core, I sobbed in gratitude the entire trip home. I felt that even if he couldn't help me physically, I was inspired and relieved because finally someone had really listened to me. After the test results came back, I realized he had listened so carefully he was able to understand what was actually happening in my body; and therefore, the true cause of my condition could be treated. That day I learned what the power of listening can do for healing.

With encouragement from a dear friend, I took my healing further by enlisting the help of a therapist—more listening—where I started learning how to listen to myself. With additional help from energetic healers, I finally discovered the emotional reason my body broke faith with my femininity. Seven years after that first appointment, I returned to my doctor for a final visit. I told him how much his careful, concerned, and thorough listening had done to help me. I shared with him that I believed a history of sexual abuse had caused me to emotionally abandon my feminine body—something that was clearly being played out physically. I don't know if he believed in the mind-body connection of emotional and physical trauma, but being true to his nature, he listened with respect and thanked me for sharing this with him.

Listening is powerful. How often are we telling the greater story, but neither we nor anyone else is listening with the depth of attention that reveals our secrets? When my mother was in the hospital and I sang to her a healing song, I have no idea if my mother consciously knew the song stimulated her healing because we never talked about it. But deep within she knew because after her healing, when her doctor came into her room, this is what she said to him: "You have no idea how much good it has done me to see my kids. I feel really good. It must have been an infection, huh?" Then she stopped her stream of uninhibited thoughts and said, "But then you are the doctor, I really shouldn't be making my own diagnosis."

Unfortunately, the doctor didn't know that if he had really listened, if he had asked a few more questions, he might have uncovered her healing secret. Instead, he said, "The penicillin must have worked for you." He assumed his treatment did the trick, though from the look on his face, you could easily see this was an unexpected outcome. Remember, he had recommended the family be called because he didn't expect her to live through the week. Her subconscious had just delivered a message. Seeing her kids helped her heal her infection.

Now I know that if any of us had known to probe and listen a little more deeply, we would have discovered love and compassion to be the real healers. If my mother and I had still been angry, resentful or hurt in our relationship, it would have been very difficult, if not impossible, to effect that kind of healing. In our mutually compassionate state and trust in one another, a doorway to energetic healing had opened.

MEDITATION

During the most stressful time of my life, I intuitively picked up a book about a man who discovered the benefits of a Jain meditation practice. That simple little book about someone's personal experiences with meditation changed my life. I was wired tight and I knew if I could teach myself to meditate, I could enjoy the serenity and peace the author described. So one morning, I got up early sat down cross-legged on my living room floor and nearly went crazy for five minutes.

I expected I wouldn't have any problem at all sitting still for twenty minutes. In reality, it was several months before I was able to quiet my itchy mind down long enough to sit still that long. Five minutes felt like an eternity when I got started. At first, just keeping myself sitting without doing anything was the challenge—never mind clearing my thoughts. Eventually, however, as my body learned to get still my thoughts did start slowing down. As my mind learned to be quiet, I experienced more and more of the luscious serenity I was craving.

In the stillness, my body started learning how to really relax. I had no idea that even when I thought I was relaxed my body was still holding tension. I didn't realize I was watching TV with my jaw tightly clenched. When I was at work my shoulders would tense up and when I worried about something my belly turned into a hardened ball. As a result of meditating, in an instant, I could tell when my body was becoming anxious or stressed. With a few meditational breaths, I could transform my tension into calm.

My shoulders stopped aching all the time. I had fewer stomachaches. Tension headaches became a condition of the past. Through meditation I was learning to notice my body. My body was speaking to me about what worked for it and what didn't. In fact, it had been talking to me all along, but I had been too busy pushing through to notice its messages. My body had to be screaming at me before I paused to listen. I had to be sick in bed before I gave my body an opportunity to relax enough to heal. Finally, as my mind grew more still, I began noticing my body communicating with me early on and could take appropriate steps to help it heal, long before I was flat on my back in bed.

Meditation, I have found, stimulates the awareness of intuitive messages. By learning to notice and listen to my body and subconscious without judgment, I was simultaneously learning how to recognize intuitive messages from my body. For example, I discovered when an activity was absolutely not going to be healthy or good for me, my stomach tensed up. Once my stomach was actually relaxed throughout the day, I could actually notice its response to a suggested activity. If a friend suggested an activity and my stomach remained relaxed, I knew the activity would probably be fine for me. If my stomach tingled a bit, I knew this would probably be really good for me.

Other places in the body can also offer intuitive awareness. You may find your heart, throat or solar plexus offer clues about what activities, relationships, circumstances, and ideas are going to be harmful or beneficial to your welfare. By first quieting the mind, then allowing the body to relax in the quiet, you can learn to notice the messages of your body. You are likely to experience constriction or tension somewhere in your body if something is potentially harmful for you or if you have some fear about the situation. If your body completely relaxes, you will probably be quite safe. If you feel happiness in your body, you will very likely enjoy a positive experience.

You will need to practice in order to understand your body's signals. For example, if you are about to go on stage in front of a lot of people, your body might tighten up in fear, but that doesn't mean the experience will be harmful for you. On the other hand, if you are an avid water skier and usually enthusiastic about skiing, but on this day your body tightens up as you think about going skiing, you might want to postpone your rendezvous with the water.

As I have become more adept with meditation, I can sometimes hear my subconscious giving messages to my conscious mind. I can actually hear what my body needs. For me, instructions often come in the form of words, such as, "electrolytes," telling me I need to give my body more electrolytes. I might receive the name of an herb to take or come out of meditation with the name of a healer in mind. I might end a meditation with the awareness I need more exercise or I might be aware of a food I need to add to or eliminate from my diet. In following the instructions of my subconscious mind, I consistently experience success in my healing. I find it to be an entirely fun way to heal, while preventing more serious conditions from occurring.

When I am meditating specifically in regard to healing, sometimes I simply ask a question and become quiet, eliminating any predetermined notion about what the answer should be. Sometimes the answer comes during or immediately after the meditation. Sometimes it is days before I receive the insight I am seeking. The answer consistently comes, and when I receive the answer, I act on the information I have received. To disregard the information is an act of disrespect or distrust of the Divine within me, so I make sure I honor and act upon the information I have received.

If I'm not getting clarity about the healing steps I need to take or I'm uncertain about information I have received, I call a friend who will meditate for or with me. This has proven to be very helpful when I seem to be drawing a blank and is quite reassuring when I am looking for clarity. Once I have received insights from a friend, I still assume my responsibility and meditate with the information they have given me for even more insight. Their awareness often primes the pump for my own inner wisdom.

Through meditation, you have an opportunity to give attention to what is really happening inside you. Meditation can provide you with powerful insights about the source of your physical and emotional pain and your healing, and yet, you may find it helpful to be aware that the purpose of meditation is not to fix yourself. Meditation is about observation—noticing what is. Learning how to meditate with pain or illness can lead to significant awareness about your own consciousness.

Eckhart Tolle, in *Practicing the Power of Now*, suggests being with what he calls the "pain-body" in the following manner: "Focus attention on the feeling inside you. Know that it is the pain-body. Don't think about it—don't let the feeling turn into thinking. Don't judge or analyze. Don't make an identity for yourself out of it. Stay present, and continue to be the observer of what is happening inside you… become aware not only of the emotional pain but also of 'the one who observes,' the silent watcher. This is the power of the Now, the power of your own conscious presence. Then see what happens."

Once the mind quiets down, you are able to perceive, hear and feel awareness from a deeper realm of consciousness. Many illnesses and injuries can be prevented, or at least dealt with immediately, when your senses are keen enough to realize what you need to be aware of to take care of yourself. Of course, for this to work, you have to trust what your senses are telling you.

A few years ago, a friend was not feeling well and asked me to do a meditation for her to discern what was making her ill. I created some time alone and went into a deep meditative trance, and as an observer I asked to know the cause of her illness. Within minutes I heard the word, "parvo" very clearly. I checked again to be sure I had heard correctly, because I knew about the parvovirus in dogs and cats, but I had never heard about it infecting humans. Once again, I received the same response to my question clearly and emphatically.

With some hesitation, I reported the results of my meditational inquiry to my friend. She listened politely, but also seemed reticent to believe what I had heard. I suggested she ask her doctor about the possibility of a human contracting parvovirus. Indeed, we discovered, there is a human parvovirus B-19, also known as the fifth disease. Her tests confirmed she had sometime earlier contracted this parvovirus.

DREAMS

As you develop your ability to relax and open your senses through meditation, you may find your dreams becoming of greater interest to you. Most of us are aware that subconscious messages often come to us through our dreams. As you create a greater opening for subconscious awareness for healing through meditation, your dreams may become even more fertile ground for subconscious messages about your health. The subconscious can provide you with either symbolic or even some very direct information about what is happening in your body.

As you understand the meaning of your own symbols in your dreams, you receive all kinds of clues about what is going on beneath the surface of your mind. These clues or symbols can provide you with information about what you need to reinforce or change in your life in order to live in health, happiness and fulfillment. A colleague, Tianna Galgano, explains in her book, *Decipher Your Dreams, Decipher Your Life*, how dreams can help you create a healthier life. "There is a better way (besides pain, illness, and putting obstacles in your path) for parts to get their point across. You can learn to talk to your inner parts, and they can learn to communicate with you…"

Imagine how much healthier you would be if the subconscious wisdom of your body and emotions spoke with you in the dreamtime, letting you know what you need for your wellness, rather than screaming at you through physical and emotional pain. Remembering, recording and interpreting your dreams can become a conduit for the inner wisdom of your subconscious to communicate directly to your conscious mind. Ask yourself a question before you go to sleep and then notice your dreams until you receive your answer.

After a few weeks of unusual intestinal discomfort I decided to find out what my inner wisdom could tell me about what was happening in my body. Before I went to sleep, I asked my subconscious mind what was going on. Early the next morning I had a dream about a big worm and this was not a garden-variety worm. Once I awoke, and before I was fully conscious, I asked my subconscious mind what the dream meant. My focus continued to drift toward my intestines. The dream was telling me I had some worms to clear out. So I talked to my doctor, described the worm and asked for recommendations for cleansing worms out of my intestinal tract.

As I developed a stronger relationship with my dreamtime I started having some inspiring dream experiences showing me there is a whole level of active subconscious involvement that can be engaged to assist with healing. I once awoke to the sound of my spirit-self singing a healing song to my body. I have even watched my spirit-hands pluck out a tumor attached to the outer wall of my uterus. Dreams have even shown me visual images of herbs to use. Each time, I knew my subconscious was aiding my conscious mind in my healing process.

In addition to giving me information about what is happening to me physically, dreams also show me what is going on emotionally. During the most depressed period of my life, my dreams were often fearful and disturbing. Now that my life is less turbulent and I am happy, my dreams are inspiring and stimulating. By observing, recording, interpreting and reflecting on my dreams, I have received a great deal of subconscious information that has helped me steer my life in positive and healthier directions. At first I thought it was a lot of bother and took too much time to record and consider my dreams, but I soon realized I was receiving valuable insights about what was really motivating my decisions. If I determined fear was the motivating force in a dream then I knew I had some emotional healing to tend to if I wanted my life to move in a more positive direction. If I knew joy was motivating me in the dream, I could relive the feeling of the dream over and over, using the memory of the feeling to inspire my life.

My husband and I share significant dreams and our interpretations of them with each other every day on our morning walk together. Because we share what is happening in the dreamtime we both have some understanding regarding what our partner is concerned about, or is inspired to do, or wants to celebrate. The understanding we develop keeps us aware of the other person's need for a little compassion, support or acknowledgement throughout the day.

LISTENING TO YOUR LANGUAGE

The other day I was on the phone with a client. She finished sharing with me a significant challenge in her life, and then considered some ways she might address that challenge to create the life she really wanted. She closed by saying, "I guess all you can really do is try, right?"

I suggested this in return. "What if you didn't try? What if you just did it?" My client didn't understand so I explained to her the word *try* inherently limited her ability to succeed. If you try, the word itself implies putting in effort without guaranteeing success. Trying, though commonly stated in regard to healing oneself, is really a waste of energy. Why try at all if you are willing to accept any outcome? Here is what is likely to happen if you decided to try. Initially you might begin to heal and as the healing requires more clarity of focus, diligence and belief, you get tired and give up. Or if you aren't seeing results fast enough you give up. Or you begin to doubt that it is really working. In any case, because *try* implies your efforts might or might not work, your healing progress slides and your worst fears are confirmed. Whatever you were doing didn't work. Now you can tell yourself, "I tried, but it didn't work."

Remember Yoda's instructions to Luke in *Star Wars* when he was learning how to levitate objects. When Yoda instructed Luke to levitate his ship out of the water, Luke told Yoda he would *try* to do it. Yoda instructed him, "Do, or do not. There is no try." Whether you are levitating your space ship or healing your body, the same principle applies. These aren't just inspiring words from a good movie script. These are words for life. Remember, when it comes to healing, trying is a waste of your energy. If you want to heal, commit your mind, body and heart to making that outcome a reality, and *do*.

Of course, some healing methodologies are going to work better for you than others. In most cases, you are going to need to give one methodology enough of a chance to know for sure. While you are utilizing a healing methodology, if you are willing to check your *try* or *do* motivation level, this will give you an indication about whether your heart and soul are behind the healing method you have chosen. If you are only trying, no method is likely to work well for you. If you are truly committed to doing and the method is only marginally effective, you may indeed need a methodology that better suits you.

Another concept that prevents people from healing is, "I really want to, but…" Anytime you use the word *but* in a sentence in regard to your healing you have probably made your excuse for not doing what is necessary to heal. In other words, you have just made your decision not to heal. Most of the time your excuse is going to be legitimate. However, your willingness to live with and accept your excuse as your reality keeps you from healing. For example, maybe you have heard about a successful treatment program for Chronic Fatigue Syndrome. You would like to receive the treatment and you don't have the money. Your statement about this might be, "I would really like to receive the treatment, *but* I can't afford it."

The statement is true, yet limiting. Consider opening the energy by shifting the statement to "I want to receive the treatment, *and* I need to figure out a way to afford it." Can you see how a simple little word and the thought that followed it changed the entire energy of the situation? Now, you might find yourself contacting the service provider to see if they have special programs for people on a limited budget. You might investigate grants for medical treatment, or ask some friends to help you out. Your creativity is expanding your horizons and working toward solutions.

Become a student of your own words. Your words reflect your doubts as well as your hopes. If doubt is in there at all, you are as likely to manifest your doubt as your hope. Once you hear what you are saying, you can begin consciously choosing new and positive words that will help erase the doubts, and reinforce your healing. You might even find it helpful to empower friends you trust to remind you when you are using language that invokes doubt. You can even use their assistance to create new statements that reinforce your commitment to ultimately becoming well.

Chapter Two — Step Two
The Restorative Power of Natural Rhythms

One of the great ironies of healing is that in order to accelerate your healing, you have to slow down.

When I ask a client about how often they spend time in nature and they reply, "Rarely," I know before we are going to get very far in a healing session, my client needs to get in touch with their own natural rhythms. Black Elk, a powerful Sioux medicine man, is known to have given a mattress to someone seeking his help in healing, then tell them to begin by spending several days resting and sleeping under a tree. He understood the importance of re-establishing natural rhythms before beginning healing work. Natural rhythms are slower than our usual hurried pace, and are more conducive to natural healing methodologies.

Natural Rhythms

It is a common misunderstanding that earth is a thing we live on to be used to serve our needs. Earth is as alive as we are and we are living in symbiotic relationship with her. When we lose touch with that awareness, we begin living on top of her instead of with her. When this happens we can easily lose touch with our natural rhythms and cycles. Symptoms of being out of sync with our natural cycles, also known as circadian rhythms, include stress, physical tension, emotional frustration, depression...and all of these can contribute to ongoing illness.

The effects of being out of balance with natural circadian cycles is explained in a white paper by Apollo Health Incorporated: "In reality circadian rhythms control the timing, quantity and quality of the hormones and neurotransmitters the body produces and eventually secretes. Hormones and neurotransmitters are the elements that determine how we feel, our sleep patterns, our appetite, our sex drive and other sleep and mood-related issues. When functioning properly, our circadian rhythms create circadian balance. When out of balance, quantity, quality and timing of hormone and neurotransmitter secretion suffer and our bodies suffer from a circadian rhythm disorder (CRD)."

One of the most powerful ways I have found to get in sync with my natural circadian rhythms is to spend time in nature. It sounds profoundly simple, and it is. When I have been working late nights, getting little sleep, obsessing about my work, and basically over-doing it, the best natural medicine I have discovered is to get out of the house, out of the car, and put my feet on Mother Earth.

I remember being so tense at one point in my life I would get angry with anyone who suggested I needed a break. I was getting more and more uptight and progressively more ill, but I was addicted to feeling needed and kept on pushing. I was avoiding my feelings and fears of unworthiness by over-working, all the while spending less time in a natural, normal, peaceful rhythm, and so I was becoming increasingly depressed and physically sick.

Eventually my desperate need to get out of my depressed state led me to finding a quiet park or forest where I could walk for hours. Periodically, I sobbed, pounded my fist on the ground, laughed, talked to myself, and eventually settled down enough to begin breathing in the scent of the trees. The more I settled in to nature, the more relief my heart found from its pain. The natural elements became my medicine. I would sit or stand still while I contemplated a stream or admired the clouds passing by me. I would lift up the head of a flower and drink in its sweet scent. Sometimes I pulled off my shoes and waded in the water or wandered about on soft grass. I loved to watch the squirrels, imitate bird sounds, crunch up dead leaves in my hands or just feel the wind on my face. And standing in the sun was like getting my battery recharged.

After releasing the burdens of my heart, I found solace in Mother Earth. In her, my appreciation for and vigor in life was renewed, and I could go on again for another day. In this natural rhythm I existed in harmony with all living things. By giving myself permission to release and then to rest in relationship with Mother Earth I restored my equilibrium in life. Here I found peace. That peace was such a relief to me, I spent more and more time outdoors with Mother Earth. The more time I spent, the more I healed my aching heart until eventually it no longer ached at all.

THE PATH OF LEAST RESISTANCE

In addition to giving you a place in which to re-establish your natural rhythms, Mother Earth teaches you to avoid pain by finding the path of least resistance. Watch water as it rushes through familiar paths. Certainly it wears down the edges of its path, eventually even wearing down hard granite surfaces, yet nonetheless, it flows in the path of least resistance. Watch a predator hunt its prey. It does not hunt the fastest in a herd. The predator hunts the slowest and weakest member. It chooses the path of least resistance. Examine the roots of a plant or tree. When the roots contact extremely hard soil or rock, the roots simply grow around the hard surface. They do not try to break through the rock or solid terrain.

These lessons may seem extremely simple, yet how often have you described yourself as "beating your head against a brick wall"? Nature doesn't do this. Humans, with our misguided egos and over-exercised wills attempt to force ourselves to live in untenable situations. We wear our bodies and our emotions down unnecessarily and then wonder why we are not feeling well.

I remember continuing to drink coffee long after I knew my body wasn't processing it very well. It made my stomach too acidic, yet I stubbornly continued to drink. Is there a lifestyle choice you cling to, although you know it isn't healthy for you? Do you continue to smoke cigarettes, drink too much alcohol, use drugs to excess, stay in jobs that make you unhappy and tense, allow a parent to keep making you angry while you continue to call regularly, argue with your spouse about unimportant matters, use sex to manipulate rather than to love, stay in abusive relationships, don't get the help you need or disrespect the help you do receive, over-work, expose yourself to chemicals you know are dangerous without adequate protection—all of it forcing your body and emotions to stretch beyond reasonable expectations? Humans, unlike other creatures of nature, frequently find and live in paths of greatest resistance.

In woundedness and fear, you may find yourself making choices that are addictive, depressing, and unhealthy. When you can't stand the pain you have created any longer, you may find yourself hoping and praying someone will take you out of your misery and fix you. If you are serious about being fixed, the key to your wellness lies in healing the wounds and assuaging the fears that live at the source of your choices. To heal emotional wounds, you will want to understand them and then soothe them with the gentle hand of your love and compassion. In order to heal you will make greater progress when you decide to stop being so hard on yourself and choose easier, kinder ways to live your life. If you choose to find personal paths of least resistance, where you are living in harmony with life, you experience far greater health and happiness.

Because we often want the instant gratification we may be inclined to sacrifice our long-term welfare. Therefore, finding a means to provide a healthier form of instant gratification, while also tending to long-term benefit can be helpful. A friend of mine who needed to lose weight, and who had been on many diets throughout her life, found a clever way to address her short-term gratification need along with her greater, long-term need of losing weight. She was particularly addicted to sweets, so in the morning, she cut up some carrots and fruits to munch on throughout the day. She placed the fruits strategically in her refrigerator—right up front on the shelf easiest to see and reach. Whenever she had a craving for something sweet, she went over the refrigerator and snacked on the carrots or fruit. To her delight, she discovered she only needed a few bites to satiate her sweet tooth, so throughout her diet she was eating healthier sweets, and fewer sweets overall. By eating food from the Mother, and acknowledging both her instant and long-term gratification needs, she found a path of least resistance that ultimately brought her greater physical health.

Mother Earth, by her very nature, through her rhythms, teaches you how to live in more harmonious ways. Being in nature helps you put your life into perspective so you can experience a softer, gentler view toward yourself and others. Notice how problems seem more manageable after you take a good walk, hike or run outdoors. Your endorphins are up, hopefully you have been breathing good air, and you have been allowing yourself to receive nourishment from the beauty of the outdoors. A walk through a rose garden can lift your spirits within minutes as you enjoy the intoxicating scent of the flowers. Take a cup of tea outside and let the breeze tickle your hair. Notice how quickly you rest into the moment when you leave your demanding world for even a few minutes and breathe with nature. After being in nature you may find yourself in a marvelous state of being that is simultaneously relaxed and energized, and therefore, in a much better frame of mind to address the daily challenges to find harmonious solutions.

RESTORATION

You are likely to become quite calm when sitting next to a gentle stream, a tranquil lake or an ocean beach. The negative ions from the water help you relax, and so does the lulling movement of the water. One of the best, simple descriptions of negative ions I found is by Denise Mann in an article in *WebMD* reviewed by Brunilda Nazario, MD for its medical accuracy: "Negative ions are odorless, tasteless, and invisible molecules that we inhale in abundance in certain environments. Think mountains, waterfalls, and beaches. Once they reach our bloodstream, negative ions are believed to produce biochemical reactions that increase levels of the mood chemical serotonin, helping to alleviate depression, relieve stress, and boost our daytime energy."

In fact quite a bit of medical research has been done demonstrating that negative ions help us simultaneously relax, reduce stress and energize us. Ecstatic, Ltd. in the United Kingdom commissioned a review of literature on the effects of air ions and concluded: "The consensus of the literature reviewed is that environmental air ion concentration levels and balance can affect a wide range of biological organisms, including humans. Elevated negative air ion levels are widely reported to have beneficial effects on humans including enhanced feeling of relaxation, and reduced tiredness, stress levels, irritability, depression, and tenseness." Putting yourself in the presence of negative ions on a regular basis can teach you how to enter into and maintain a relaxed state, which can in turn can help you experience more lasting healing.

The Mother brings you into balance, helps you find your equilibrium, and pulls you into an ancient, soothing rhythm that is natural to humans—perhaps forgotten and even resisted in our fast-paced lives—but quite natural. As you step into nature, the mind begins to quiet and the body slows down. Your body finally has an opportunity to begin doing its repair work. The body is no longer having to crank out enough adrenaline to keep you going. It can focus on functions of the body that need restorative attention.

If you are unwell, your eight or fewer hours of sleep a night are probably not enough restful hours for your body to do the work it needs to do. If you are chronically ill and healing over time, sleeping all day is usually not very satisfying to the mind and spirit or your body. Finding a calm rhythm and pace by which to live out your day is one way to help your body and mind rest enough to continue repairing while you are engaged in life, and nature can help you get in touch with that rhythm.

If you work in an office without windows or in a building that looks out on other buildings, I suggest bringing plants and stones into your workspace. If you are not very close to nature, bring nature close to you. You might even consider a small water fountain for your desk. When you start feeling stressed at work, pause for a moment, breathe into your body until the muscles relax, listen to the fountain, hold a stone and rub your thumb across it, gaze softly at your plant and watch your entire body and mental state shift. When you feel calm, approach your next task from that relaxed space and notice how much more effectively you complete your work.

Many years ago I started my own consulting company. I had never been self-employed, so I frequently found myself feeling scared and nervous, especially when I had no clients. I made it a practice to sit down in front of my sliding glass door that looked out on to a sweet little patio with flowers in pots and a nearby tree bending over the privacy fence to shade one of the chairs. I observed nature and breathed until my entire body and mind were completely soothed. When I felt a happy, peaceful disposition, I returned to my desk and resumed my work.

I refused to let my fear take over. I refused to let it make me doubtful. And I especially refused to let my bodily tension and mental anxiety make me sick. Instead, I faced my fears head on. I calmed the beast within me until I knew I could continue working from a positive perspective. After breathing with nature, when my body was relaxed, I worked most efficiently. I told myself the work I was doing was getting me ready for my clients. Soon I would be so busy attending to client needs, these other office tasks would be difficult to accomplish, so I'd best get them done now.

As I predicted, in very little time, I was quite busy with clients. And whenever a client asked me to do work for him or her that was new to me or a stretch for me, I resumed the same process whenever I felt my fears arise. I still had my challenges; however, I had learned that keeping my body and mind calm—in a natural rhythm—helped me restore and maintain health and productivity even through the most difficult situations.

In order to maintain that balance, I walked in the park every day, exercised, ate well and enjoyed each day. On weekends, I would take long hikes to help me clear my mind. Some weekdays, I would stop at a flower garden or the boardwalk along the river and breathe in fresh perspective. I allowed myself to find comfort in the rhythms of Mother Earth. I even gave myself permission to enjoy the power of spending days at a time alone, in the restorative solitude of the Mother. With multi-day retreats close to the Earth, I had plenty of time to release the pressures and demands of a clock-driven world and to enjoy the natural rhythms of sunrise, sunset and vast world of natural events in between.

Recently a friend reminded me about a healing experience he had shortly after he met me. He had joined me and others for a week of spiritual activities out in the woods and was looking forward to the time to retreat and help in camp. Being in good spirits, he jumped across a nearby creek and landed in such a way that he hurt his back, so much so that he came back into camp bent over. I asked him if he would like me to do some sound medicine for him and though this was very new to him, he agreed.

He explained to me sometime later that even though this was a brand new experience for him, he decided to let go of any beliefs that might have limited his experience and opened himself fully to the healing it might provide for him. He made a clear decision to let go of the injury, connected to Source, entered in to a meditative state and listened to the sounds. Though others offered massage, he was too tender to be touched, so we continued with more sound medicine on the second day. Between sessions he gave his body permission to relax, letting the sounds do their job. By the third day, he was regaining mobility.

Though he was deeply disappointed that his activities were limited, instead of becoming angry, he meditated quietly on what was happening for him. One of his learning opportunities during this time was to allow others to help him. He believes this is one of the gifts that came from his injury. Now when he needs help in his life, he asks for it, remembering the caring support he was given by everyone in the camp. When he returned home he received help from a chiropractor and continued his practice of meditation and relaxation. He told me he continues this practice whenever he has any back pain and can still hear the sounds I sang to him during that week several years ago. His practice allows him to heal immediately, and when he does this regularly, he believes he keeps his back healthy and strong.

In my experience, healing doesn't work very well when it is rushed or pushed. Healing occurs when you have slowed down enough to observe what is really going on. Healing starts happening immediately when you replace negative feelings by nurturing feelings of compassion. You heal when you are able to relax in that compassion, allowing your body to receive what you need in a form that is healthy. It happens when your subconscious and conscious minds are comfortably in complete alignment with a single focus of healing.

It takes more than a strong will to heal. I have attempted several times to heal myself by simply thinking with conviction, "My body is healthy. I am completely well," and then went about my business as usual. Don't get me wrong. I absolutely believe in the power of affirmation. What I have come to know is that the more I feel what I am affirming, and the deeper from my subconscious the affirmation comes, the more effective the affirmation and eventually the healing. Further, the more the affirmation is like an alluring invitation, the greater the probability my own conscious and subconscious awareness will accept what I am suggesting. If I want to access my subconscious deeply, if I really want to connect with the consciousness of the cells in my body, I've got to be relaxed, preferably in a trance state. The more relaxed I am, the deeper my trance-like state—the greater the access, and the more responsive the body becomes.

If a trance state seems strange to you, you might find it helpful to realize we go in and out of different kinds of trance states throughout the day. Spacing out when driving is a form of trance or hypnotic state, as is daydreaming. Unlike what you might have seen on television or at a magic show, it is a natural state in which you are fully in control. The deeply relaxed state brings with it a heightened sensitivity and focus that is helpful in affirming positive change.

Dr. Andrew Weil recommends hypnotherapy for a variety of conditions where the body will be helped by a hypnotic state in which appropriate suggestions can be made to the subconscious mind of the patient to promote healing. In an article for *Transformation Works* out of Tucson, Arizona, he describes the benefits of a trance state: "Essentially, trance is an altered state of consciousness marked by decreased scope and increased intensity of awareness. What distinguishes hypnotherapy is that it involves a deliberate choice to enter this state of consciousness for a goal beyond relaxation: to focus your concentration and use suggestion to promote healing. It can be done in person with a hypnotherapist or you can do it yourself, called self-hypnosis."

In my own experience with hypnosis, I enter into a trance-like state comparable to the one I enter in meditation. It is also very much akin to the deep serenity I feel when I am breathing with and resting in nature. For me it is like being in the rhythmic pulse of a gently ebbing lake. Everything around me, all of my usual distractions are still there, but greatly minimized, as my full and complete attention is drawn into this inward state.

The suggestions offered in that conscious state, or better yet, coming from my subconscious awareness, invite me to open my mind, body and spirit to better choices, beliefs and perspectives. Even in self-induced trance states, I am gently coaxing my subconscious mind to consider a healthier belief system. In this tranquil yet heightened state of awareness it is easier for me to accept, with much less resistance than normal, the thoughtful and loving guidance of healing perspective.

Keeping up a stressful pace, remaining disconnected from nature, and using my mind to will myself well, only exacerbate illness. This is how I approached healing for the first 28 years of my life, and I was a pretty unhealthy adult. And I've met countless people using the same strategy unsuccessfully. Healing is an act of surrender rather than an attempt to gain more control. I began healing significantly when I started surrendering to a greater wisdom than my will. I had to relax into myself, allowing inner wisdom and guidance to emerge. And one of the greatest teachers of relaxation is Mother Earth. There is a reason many of us seek nature when we go on vacation.

When you find your rhythm with Mother Earth, you stop working so hard at life. You stop living in the place of most resistance and live from a place of least resistance. You slide into a natural rhythm, a more relaxed rhythm that helps you maintain health, promote healing, and allows you to regain healthy equilibrium. In this state, your body and mind naturally begin working with you to restore and enhance your health. The formula is simple. You don't get to physical health, inner peace or joy through stress and tension. If you are like me, you have probably already tried that method, and it doesn't work. You have to be willing to find a relaxed and natural pace, in harmony with the natural rhythms of life. That is where you will find joy and contentment, while giving your body and emotions every opportunity to heal.

PETS

Numerous scientific studies have been done proving the benefits of having pets in lowering blood pressure. In fact, pets are more apt to help lower your blood pressure than interaction with spouses and friends. This is true for adults, children and the elderly. Talking to a pet, stroking one, or even being around a pet is known to lower your blood pressure. And studies using both cats and dogs do not seem to indicate that it makes a difference whether your companion is a feline or canine. High blood pressure, according to recent estimates from the American Heart Association, affects about one-third of adults in the U.S. Further the AHA states: "Uncontrolled high blood pressure can lead to stroke, heart attack, heart failure or kidney failure."

Cardiovascular health benefits too, if you own a dog, because dog owners tend to take more frequent walks. Imagine holding a cat in your lap and feeling it purr against you. It creates an immediately calming bond between the two of you. Watching fish swim in a fish tank is profoundly relaxing. Some studies even indicate pets may have a direct influence on increasing your life span. Pet owners will tell you their pets can provide a distraction from the pain or tension they are experiencing. Pets can make a tremendous difference in helping you increase your frequency of outdoor exercise, distracting you from your discomfort, or slowing down your heart rate and blood pressure for greater health.

Emotionally you may find yourself responding to life's challenging situations a lot better if you have a pet in your life, simply because you experience less stress. I remember a friend telling me she got her dog after leaving a marriage where she experienced little affection. She soon discovered the life-giving experience of sharing affection with her pet companion, which ultimately prepared her for receiving and giving affection with her current husband. In watching her with her husband now, you wouldn't easily know that exchanges of affection were ever an issue in her life.

Of course if you are allergic to animals or you have acquired the wrong type of pet for your personality, the presence of that pet is likely to increase stress in your life. By the way, if you have never owned a pet, puppies and kitties require a lot of attention and tend to be very high energy. If you are looking for a pet to help you relax, consider finding an older dog or cat from a shelter, or buy some fish from a local pet store. If you are thoughtful and judicious about choosing the right pet for you, you can experience greater physical and emotional benefits through their stress reducing influence.

Nourishment

Yearly, I meet with friends someplace in the woods where we camp in tents, living very close to Mother Earth for a week. I have noticed there is something about being outside with the Mother that seems to inspire us to live more healthily. We frequently take hikes together, spend long hours sitting quietly alone with a book or a flute, laugh heartily and regularly, and generally—slow down. I have also noticed we seem to eat better. Oh sure, a little bit of junk food finds it way into the cars, but when someone puts out a bag of potato chips on the table and someone else puts out a bag of baby carrots, the carrots are likely to be devoured long before the chips. Though people have brought some naturally sweetened sodas with them, you rarely see a can in anyone's hands, but you do see plenty of water bottles within reach. It seems to me just being with Mother Earth can inspire us to eat and drink what comes from her naturally.

Some friends of mine created their own organic garden on their property. They tended it daily and enjoyed gathering their small harvests as each plant was ready to be picked. One of them shared with me the experience of eating food that was completely mature and ripe before it was harvested. He said, "You know how you can eat a salad and walk away from the table hungry?" I knew exactly what he meant. It had happened to me many times. "Well," he said, "when the plant is mature and you it eat, you are getting all of its nutrients, so a simple salad is completely filling and satisfying, plus the vegetables and fruit taste naturally sweet and full of flavor."

I discovered the same to be true of natural spring water. It tends to be a little bit sweet and is full of good flavor, and good spring water is actually filling in addition to being refreshing. I can hardly stand to drink most tap water because it tastes like chemically purified water, and of course it is chemically treated water. No wonder so many people I know don't drink water. If unfiltered tap water were my only source, I probably wouldn't drink it either.

A lot is being written today about the benefits of eating organic food and the importance of drinking good water in maintaining health. I'm not going to expound on their health benefits here, but as an observer, I have come to believe what we put into our bodies affects our bodies. If we want to feel healthy, it behooves us to eat healthy food. Our bodies were designed to eat what the Mother provides. It just makes sense to eat from her table. In my own experience and observations, simply spending more time outdoors stimulates a desire to eat better food and drink healthier water. Food with vitality brings vitality into our bodies.

CHAPTER THREE — STEP THREE
THE HEALING MAGIC OF CREATIVITY

Creativity focuses you away from the pain and engages you in creating new life for yourself over and over again.

Engaging your creativity rejuvenates you and keeps you involved in life in positive ways. You might even find yourself forgetting about your pain for long periods of time when you are involved in a creative endeavor. You may find that creativity helps you discover pathways to eliminating illness and pain completely. As you engage your creativity, your intuitive abilities could increase as you inspire your mind and soul to look at life from different perspectives. Intuition can lead you to a clearer understanding about what you need to do to transform pain and suffering into happiness and joy.

RELEASING THE PAIN
THROUGH CREATIVE EXPRESSION

There I was sitting on my couch with a sketchpad and a box of crayons. I drew something that seemed really stupid so I ripped it out and threw it away. I had no idea what to draw after that so I didn't draw anything. I was tense and agitated, so I got up and started cleaning my apartment. In the depths of my depression, I found cleaning the house was good therapy for me. As I cleaned, thoughts and feelings drifted in and out of me. I had learned to let them drift. But every now and then, one of them lingered—usually some painful feeling about the past.

That day, one of those feelings grabbed my attention. Deep sorrow was welling up seemingly out of nowhere. As tears filled my eyes, I walked over to the pad and crayons. I coached myself not to think. "Just draw whatever comes without judgment," I told myself.

Amidst the tears, I drew child-like images, most without any readily apparent meaning. When finished, I felt relieved. After taking a couple of deep breaths, I put on my coat and went out for a walk to help me continue clearing my mind and emotions. When I returned home I took a good look at the images. I knew they were basically representations of feelings—feelings I believed I had known well all my life. I wrote words next to the images and noted how my emotions had shifted from anxious to peaceful in my process of drawing. My agitated feelings were gone, replaced by serenity. Whatever needed to be felt had been felt and had passed through me, leaving my body relaxed, and feeling healthy and energetic.

In my case, creativity became a way to explore the root of my emotional unrest and depression. I have also used creativity to discover and explore the unconscious beliefs behind states of physical illness. Simply by getting still, focusing on the place in my body most in pain and making sounds intuitively, I have discovered a world of insights about the emotional feelings, and ultimately the beliefs, limiting my ability to feel well. Once I fully express the sounds of the pain, the sounds change automatically, without me consciously directing them. Then naturally, new soothing, calming sounds emerge, eventually leading me to sounds that actually bring about physical healing.

Creative expression can become a safe place for expressing and even transforming emotions. Bottled-up emotions we ignore can become fertile ground for oppression. You might think about it this way—suppression results in oppression. Imagine the toll your body takes every time you suppress your feelings and then act out your hurt and anger by being hard on yourself. When life feels like the pits, your body is likely feeling the same way.

When I was suppressing my feelings, I was depressed. I acted out that depression in anger, disgust with myself and my family, cynicism, sarcasm, gossip, and caustic remarks to people I loved. Oh, I was expressing feelings all right, but I wasn't acknowledging the deeper sorrow, regret, guilt and fear that were actually driving my life. I oppressed myself by being so hard on myself. I oppressed others by being hard on them. My personal oppression showed in my body with constant aches and pains, unbalanced hormones, low energy, and a weak immune system. The release from my cycle came when I acknowledged those suppressed feelings in appropriate ways. Therapy was one way I was able to safely explore my deeper feelings; creativity was another.

CREATIVITY REMINDS US
NOTHING HAS TO BE FOREVER

Creativity can lead you into a journey of discovery about natural order. In the natural order of life, all things change. Forest floors that have been damaged by fire eventually become fertile ground for new seedlings. Within years, new life grows where there once was only destruction. The same is true with our emotions and illness. Our current state of emotions does not have to be a permanent one. Neither does illness, though it may feel that way at times. This is especially true with chronic pain. It is easy to believe you will always feel pain, and you may find yourself doubting you can ever be free from that pain. However, you have a consciousness that can invite your body to enjoy greater ease, and you can use your creativity to guide your physical energy toward comfort and freedom.

When you follow your creative impulses without judgment, you naturally experience death and birth, pain and joy, sorrow and happiness moving through your creative expression. Whether your preferred form of creativity is visual art, music, dance, acting, writing, sewing, cooking or any other artistic endeavor, one minute of your expression may look very different from the next minute's expression. As you explore your creativity, you discover the ongoing changes of your body, emotions, mind and spirit. Nothing is static. You are constantly changing in response to your feeling in the moment. In terms of physical and emotional health, this could translate as, "I might be in pain in this moment, but in the next, I could feel completely comfortable and free."

When healing from chronic conditions, the reminder that you can indeed feel good again is very important. Your body is sending you an overriding message of pain most of the time. If you want to change your reality from pain to feeling good, you will want to invite and lovingly convince your mind and body that this is possible. One of the best ways to remind yourself that pain does not have to be a static condition is to explore the natural order of constant change through creative expression.

INSPIRATION CAN ALLEVIATE PAIN

Healing often consumes you. Learning how to get well and eliminate the pain can feel like, and often is, a full-time job. While you might not feel up to making your mark on the world or creating your legacy, exercising your creativity can provide you with inspiration to continue healing.

Some years ago, a friend of mine was suffering from a condition that created chronic pain for her. Each day, she put significant energy into healing and feeling good. However, pain has a way of constantly tapping you on the shoulder like an unforgiving friend. She needed a way to get her mind off the pain—a place where she could become so absorbed she could forget about her challenges for a while. Knowing her talents I suggested something she could create with her hands. In no time, her hands were moving, her mind was occupied, and for moments she was enjoying life without pain. As she began to feel better, my friend actually started selling the items she made at house parties and on-line. Her home-based business provided her with a place to focus her mind that provided freedom from her pain, allowed her to be of service to others, and supplement her income. Most of all, every moment she experienced free from pain inspired her to create more moments free from pain.

Research supports my friend's experience as seen in this article from *Science Daily*, which discusses the effects of art therapy with 50 cancer patients. "A study published in the *Journal of Pain and Symptom Management* found that art therapy can reduce a broad spectrum of symptoms related to pain and anxiety in cancer patients. In the study done at Northwestern Memorial Hospital, cancer patients reported significant reductions in eight of nine symptoms measured by the Edmonton Symptom Assessment Scale (ESAS) after spending an hour working on art projects of their choice."

Providing patients with a variety of subject matter and media, the study measured the effects of art therapy on pain, tiredness, nausea, depression, anxiety, drowsiness, lack of appetite, well-being and shortness of breath. Nausea was the only symptom that did not seem to improve with art therapy. In fact, some patients stated the art therapy had actually energized them.

Music is another art form that has been studied in relationship to reducing pain. According to a paper in the *Journal of Advanced Nursing*, researchers carried out a controlled clinical trial with 60 people, dividing them into two music groups and a control group. They found that people who listened to music for an hour every day for a week reported improved physical and psychological symptoms compared to the control group. They determined that: "Listening to music can reduce chronic pain by up to 21 per cent and depression by up to 25 per cent…. It can also make people feel more in control of their pain and less disabled by their condition."

Listening to enchanting, uplifting music for a while can energize and soothe your body, mind and spirit, giving you respite from pain, and it can even help you heal. In his book, *The Mozart Effect*, Don Campbell discusses various clinically proven physiological effects music can have in the healing process, including increasing endorphins (the natural opiates of the body), stimulating the immune system, regulating stress-hormone levels, affecting body temperature, strengthening memory and even enhancing endurance. Music, like many forms of creativity, is good for more than entertainment, it promotes healing.

THE MAGIC OF HUMOR

One of the more famous stories about healing through humor comes from Dr. Norman Cousins. In 1964 he was being treated in the hospital for ankylosing spondylitis, a progressive degenerative disease, creating excruciatingly painful inflammation. With his doctor's agreement, he checked out of the hospital and began experimenting with humor to see if it would alter his body chemistry in a positive manner. Dr. Cousins watched Marx Brothers' films and read books that inspired him to laugh. This is what he learned: "I made the joyous discovery that ten minutes of genuine belly laughter had an anesthetic effect and would give me at least two hours of pain-free sleep."

In 1979, he wrote his book, *The Anatomy of an Illness*, where he reported the value of humor in his recovery from this rare and debilitating disease. Today you can find countless articles and studies on the value of humor in healing. Of course, you can also become an observer of your own experiences. Incorporate more laughter in your day and notice how you feel.

Many studies have demonstrated the benefits of humor on heath. Here is one that specifically shows us how humor positively effects healthy functioning of blood cells. In a research study done at the University of Maryland School of Medicine, researchers determined that: "Laughter appears to cause the tissue that forms the inner lining of blood vessels, the endothelium, to dilate or expand in order to increase blood flow."

According to the principal investigator, Michael Miller, MD, Director of Preventative Cardiology at the University Medical Center: "The endothelium is the first line in the development of atherosclerosis or hardening of the arteries, so given the results of our study, it is conceivable that laughing may be important to maintain a healthy endothelium, and reduce the risk of cardiovascular disease."

To put this in perspective, the U.S. Department of Health and Human Services tells us one in three women dies of heart disease. According to the Centers for Disease Control and Prevention, heart disease is the number one cause of death among men. Obviously, reducing your risk of heart disease means you just might live longer.

In this same study at the University of Maryland School of Medicine, the researchers tested the effects of stress on blood vessels. They showed alternating funny and disturbing movies to their test volunteers, and then measured the effects. After watching stressful movies, their endothelium constricted to reduce blood flow. While the researchers aren't sure exactly what part of laughter caused dilation instead of constriction, perhaps the physical act of laughing or a release of endorphins, they do know laughter affects blood vessels.

Now, let me encourage you to notice all the funny things that happen in your world every day. I decided some years ago that the reason I make mistakes is so I will have something to laugh about. I used to be one of the most serious people I know, and I wasn't feeling too well physically or emotionally when I was so dour. I used to run right over someone's funny remark in order to talk about what I thought was much more important and significant. When I began understanding

34

the importance of humor, I taught myself to stop my monologue long enough to hear what they said and let the humor sink in. Then I would chuckle, eventually returning to what I was saying. Over time, I learned to really enjoy the funny remarks because I discovered there was often more wisdom in the humor than there was in my seriousness. The more I have learned to laugh, the more I have learned to enjoy life.

DISCOVERING YOUR INTUITION THROUGH YOUR INSPIRATION

As you become more creative, your intuition is going to be stimulated. It is a natural process. In order to be truly creative, you open to the well of inspiration within you. Guess where your intuition lives? It lives in that same body of inspiration. Listen to a creative person or intuitive talk about their work. My husband is a composer. If I ask him why he created a certain passage of music, I know from experience he is probably going to tell me at some point in our conversation that it "sounds right and *feels right*." He describes his choice through his senses and feelings. One of my closest friends is a skilled intuitive and investor. If I ask her why she is considering a certain investment, she starts out my telling me the logical reasons she thinks this investment is a good one. She finishes up by telling me whether or not it *feels right* to her.

When my husband and my friend tell me something *feels right* they are responding from their intuition. Creativity and intuition both come from inspiration, so when you stimulate your creativity you simultaneously stimulate your intuition because you are ultimately energizing the far greater sphere of inspiration. When your inspiration is stimulated you start paying attention to signals from within—senses, feelings and impressions.

Perhaps you are planting a flower garden in your front yard. You have researched plants that grow well in your region, soil conditions, plants that need shade and sun, and watering requirements. You have considered which plants will grow to be tall and which ones remain low to the ground, which ones flower and which ones do not. You have purchased your plants and now you are looking at the flowerbed. Even if you planned out where every plant would go, at some point, inspiration is probably going to kick in, if you let it. You might sense one flower is going to look better next to a certain bush, or a certain arrangement of colors is more pleasing, or you decide a few more tall plants would look better in a certain spot. Or maybe you have all the plants in perfect places, but you realize something is missing. You decide it needs a fountain or birdbath. Your garden might even change over years as you let your inspiration guide you into creating beauty.

Just like creating a garden, your inspiration can play a significant role in your healing journey, if you open to it. You might be inspired to go to a weekend retreat, finally giving yourself some quiet reprieve and rest from the chaos of your life, which then inspires you to create fewer stressful conditions at home. You might find yourself inspired to talk to someone at a party about your renewed commitment to healing which might lead you to the perfect doctor or healing treatment. Or your inspiration could lead you to a book at the bookstore that opens up a whole new world of understanding about your healing journey. As you learn to listen and follow the wisdom of your inspiration, you discover the power of intuition.

You may have discovered the power of your intuition as a parent. Perhaps you have had one of those moments when you knew you should check on the kids, just before one of them did something that could have hurt them. Or maybe, when your child was a baby and was crying, you rocked and cuddled and sang every lullaby you knew to him or her with little result. Then from seemingly out of nowhere, you started humming something you have never heard before and the baby calmed down. Through your intuition you found sounds that were calming to your baby.

You may find your intuition to be a bit subtler than inspiration, yet when listened to and followed can lead you to safe and effective healing options, and keep you from ineffective or harmful ones. A good friend of mine called to tell me her 73-year-old mother was going to be having surgery for a hernia. She was concerned and wondered if I could pick up some intuitive insights about it. I got very still and quiet, asking my inner knowing several questions. I asked about the outcome of the surgery—it would be successful. I inquired about her mother's ability to heal after the surgery—she would heal nicely. I checked on the effects of anesthesia the doctor planned to use—there would be no harm. And finally I inquired about the ability of her mother's heart to sustain the surgery—her heart would be fine. Though I passed along the information to my friend, she still seemed very worried, calling me several times before the surgery and each time I asked the same questions, checking my intuition for the likely outcomes. Each time, the answers came back the same.

Weeks later, my friend called me quite distraught. "The surgery was successful, but the doctor removed a tiny hernia we didn't even know was there prior to her last exam, and he left the fist-sized hernia that was supposed to be removed." I felt sick. How did I miss that? As my friend pointed out, the surgery was successful. It just hadn't occurred to me to ask if the doctor was going to remove the correct hernia. She was right. I had not stretched beyond the same few questions to see what else might have been a probability.

I was so embarrassed—devastated really—that I had not done a better job for my friend and her mother. I spent days feeling guilty about it before it occurred to me to consider what I needed to learn from this event. I had not been listening carefully to my friend. She was worried, and it seemed so natural for a daughter to worry about her mother having surgery at age 73, that I wasn't listening to any other considerations that might have been behind her concern. As it turned out, my friend's own intuition was talking to her, and I misinterpreted it as worry.

My friend did some research on this doctor after the bungled surgery to find out a lawsuit had been filed against him for a similar surgery where the wrong part was removed. In this case, the patient's mental and physical health became so deteriorated after the debilitating surgery, he eventually committed suicide. Had my friend or I recognized her mistaken worry as an intuitive impulse, we might have discovered this doctor's background earlier and averted an unnecessary surgery.

DISCOVER YOUR SPIRITUAL GIFT AND YOUR PURPOSE

Because I desperately wanted to heal, I discovered my ability to heal with sound. Although my mother was the first person I sang to who had a dramatic response to my healing sounds, it was my own desire to heal myself that led me to sound in the first place. I had been a singer all my life and it had never occurred to me to use my sounds for healing until a friend suggested I consider singing to the emotional pain that lived behind the physical pain my heart was experiencing. Within days I began seeing the results of singing, or sounding, my feelings. I didn't use any words, just the sounds that seemed to correlate to what I was feeling emotionally. Deeply in the sounds, I witnessed my hidden pain as I sang the feeling of the pain. In honoring the pain itself, I observed how the sounds gradually and naturally changed until they were soothing my heart—ultimately into relief and wellness.

As I sounded my feelings, in a way improvising in the moment, I realized I had been singing intuitively since I was a child. I used to sing my younger brothers and sister to sleep humming whatever came to me. Who knows how much healing was coming through my sounds at such a young age. My parents encouraged me to sing, but they had no frame of reference for the healing properties of sound, so they didn't consider singing in this way as an indicator that I had a healing gift.

Since discovering my own gift, I have met many people who have discovered their gifts, and they usually discover them through the process of their own healing. A dear friend of mine, Krystalya Marié, discovered she could see and draw healing symbols. A woman I knew in Portland, Oregon found she could heal her body through dance. Yet another friend uncovered an affinity for crystals. She can energetically hold the energy of the crystal in her mind and see that energy in her body until her body responds by resonating with the frequency of the crystal. Still another friend can drum healing rhythms that produce measurable changes in blood pressure and bring significant healing to various illnesses.

You might know someone who has discovered their healing gift. Maybe you know your gift(s), or maybe you think you don't have one. In my experience, everyone has a gift for healing themselves. One of the benefits in healing is discovering the gift. That is why it is so important to engage your creativity. If you aren't sure, explore different modalities, or consider what you loved to do as a child. We often exhibit our healing tendencies when we are children. Krystalya Marié was shocked to discover her healing gift came through drawing because one of her parents, a professional artist, discouraged her from drawing when she was young. As soon as she gave herself permission to do what she had been told she wasn't very good at doing, her healing gift emerged.

A woman I met recently discovered her life work through her healing process while simultaneously freeing her body from pain. Her creative process is writing. When her emotions become intense, whether happiness, anger, joy, or sorrow, she writes. As she writes, her awareness transforms the feelings into an opening of profound spiritual revelation. If she shares her writing with others, she has noticed a doorway of creation seems to open up so that her desires and the desires of the listener manifest very quickly. The process has been so profound, she now shares the process itself with others.

I asked her how her body responds to her writing. After reflecting for a moment, she said, "Physically, my life becomes effortless. Energy is flowing through me freely. Stuckness and pain vanish." She then quoted one of her writings. "I give in to my joy."

Imagine discovering your life purpose and your freedom from pain simply by engaging your creativity. Imagine knowing you came into this world fully equipped with your own special healing gift. Imagine finding out your healing process could actually be fun and eventually bring you joy. Now, maybe fun sounds too far out there, but I must tell you when I am singing healing sounds for myself or someone else, there are many moments of absolute bliss and peace. The sounds are invigorating, life affirming, and fulfill me. Your gift can do the same for you.

The more you recognize and appreciate your talents and gifts, the more you will want to use them. As you serve others with the best you have to give, you are also feeding your soul—your purpose for living. Have you ever had an experience where you were so intent on helping someone else that you completely forget about your own problems or pain for a while? Have you ever felt the need to get back to work even though you have just gone through a difficult or traumatic personal experience? Have you noticed that even when you are depressed, if you make yourself get out of bed and do something for someone else you feel better? There is an urge within us that knows when we are being of service to others we feel alive, valuable, needed and fulfilled. We can experience great satisfaction in making a difference in the lives of others. Using your creative abilities and talents in the service of others will invigorate you. Tapping into your intuitive wisdom and gifts, and using them to assist others in their need will affirm the importance of your service and your life. And with a reason to live, you have a greater reason to heal.

Healing is an inspirational journey you are experiencing to remember your Divine nature. As you heal you embrace more fully who you truly are, your natural gifts, and your ability to be of greatest service to others. You discover you increasingly have the energy and desire to live and to engage life fully. You can create more freedom from pain and live your life in greater ease, and even fun, simply by embracing your creativity.

BECOMING EMPOWERED

When I told my friends I was writing this book, some of them sent me their personal stories. One beautifully empowering story came from a woman I sang to many years ago, who has lived for the past two years with chronic back pain. Attempting to find some method that would help her heal, she had been to a physical therapist, an orthopedic surgeon, a massage therapist, an acupuncturist, a chiropractor, and an osteopath. Every treatment she tried only seemed to make her condition worse.

Then one day she received a notice in the mail for a spiritual, rhythmic movement workshop. She couldn't imagine driving the many miles to get to the workshop, given she was spending most of her days lying flat. But, she told me, her intuition would not leave her alone. She knew she had to get there. Intuitively she felt the pain was related to unreleased grieving, and she knew she needed to do something to shift her emotions. So, with great effort, she made the drive and arrived at the workshop. Initially, she was unable to participate because of her great discomfort. She just sat listening to the compelling rhythms, until finally she had to get up to join them. She fully participated in the rhythmic movements for two days. This is what she said about the following day. "The third day I woke up and for the first time in two years I was pain free. I was ecstatic… I knew that I had made the decision to live and I felt that I had Divine presence, guidance to help me do this."

In her letter to me she explained why she believed she had been stuck in pain for so long. "I think that for me healing had to do with not feeling helpless which I felt when I was around the orthopedic surgeon—who did want to do surgery. I always felt as if I was powerless, even with the massage therapist or the other people I mentioned. I went to them for help. I expected them to help me, to cure me, and when they didn't I became morose....I realized I thought that by asking for help, I was admitting I couldn't do it—and that was as debilitating as the actual physical cause of my problems."

She was able to listen to her intuitive impulse and engage in the healing power of a spiritual rhythmic dance, and in her willingness to surrender to that greater wisdom, she found her freedom. This is the power of creativity. This is the power of intuition. Perhaps, most important of all, she shed her feelings of powerlessness, claiming her Divine right to live and honoring her own power to heal. She found the Divine essence within her. By accessing her Divine essence she created a miracle.

CHAPTER FOUR — STEP FOUR
CREATING MIRACLES MAY BE MORE ACCESSIBLE THAN YOU REALIZE

Miracles happen when you open to the extraordinary power of the Divine hidden inside yourself.

Like my friend in the previous chapter, many of us in our healing process look everywhere but inside for our answers. We search for doctors and healers who can make us better. We hope with all hope someone will provide us with the miracle cure. This approach can actually promote a great sense of hopelessness about our ability to have any effect on our own healing. We have to wait until the right cure comes along, wringing our hands until that moment. Hopelessness can deplete our energy, cause us to spend time and thought worrying rather than healing, and give rise to blaming others for the ineffectiveness we are feeling.

If you perceive your healing is dependent upon someone else, you have probably limited your ability to heal and recover quickly. Even if you are receiving the best treatment possible, you can accelerate your own healing by maintaining a positive perspective, engaging your creativity, relaxing your mind and body to maximize your body's natural healing potential, engaging your own energetic healing abilities, and observing subtle changes you can make to support your healing process. I have seen people leave hospitals early, simply because they used one or more of these steps.

RELEASING THE NEED TO BLAME

When we are emotionally or physically ill, it is easy to blame someone else for the discomfort or pain we are experiencing. We blame our parents for making poor choices. We blame the person who rammed into us with their car, the restaurant that poured coffee that was too hot, the doctor who didn't find a solution, our spouse, our children and God. We are so blame-oriented; the United States has more lawsuits than any other country in the world. Too often we blame others when we need to be taking responsibility for our own choices and too often we take responsibility for other people's choices when we need to be empowering others to decide for themselves. This lack of balanced perspective around blame and responsibility keeps us trapped in unhealthy dynamics of power over others, resentment, and emotional pain, resulting in subconscious resistance to healing and limited spiritual and ethical development. We would all benefit from a more balanced perspective about responsibility and blame.

Blame is interesting energy. While it might feel good to make someone else responsible, in the end, it doesn't help you heal. Blaming others for your illness or depression locks you in a loop of continued pain while you wait for someone else to ask for your forgiveness. The problem with this is that the other person may never apologize, which leaves you stuck in your pain indefinitely. If you want to engage the spiritual power of a healing journey, you need to be an active participant by taking responsibility for and fully embracing your wellness, regardless of who may have instigated the cause.

Your consciousness is steering your life when it comes to your mental and physical health. If you are angry with yourself or anyone else, true and deep healing will be impaired. Just try to have a good relationship with your parents when you are still blaming them for not being there for you when you were a child. Or imagine enjoying a great time with your partner when you are still blaming him or her for not meeting your needs. Then imagine giving yourself the physical healing attention you need when you are furious with someone else. Freedom from blame empowers you and frees your energy to be 100% in charge of your healing process.

Blame is not the same as accountability. When someone has done something inappropriate that has directly caused you to be injured, they have responsibility. It is appropriate to hold that person accountable for their choices. Blame occurs when you had some responsibility too and you want to punish them for their share of responsibility as well as your own. You can even blame yourself by punishing yourself for your share of responsibility, plus the responsibilities of others. Blame also occurs when you are making someone else responsible for your feelings and reactions. Perhaps you were abused as a child and now as an adult you blame your abuser for how you feel about yourself today. Of course you have a right to feel hurt and anger; however, blame is toxic because it usually feeds the anger with guilt and resentment. When you are blaming, every time you talk about what someone did to you, even if what happened was truly awful, the flames of blame get fanned locking in your anger and keeping you at a distance from healing.

Unfortunately, I have observed in people who have come to me for help, those who do not want to let go of the blame, contract one illness after another. Blame is such a huge impediment to deep, lasting healing that releasing it may be one of the most significant gifts you give yourself in your journey. I released a lot of my blame in therapy and through my spiritual practice. Just as I did initially, you may feel justified in your feelings of blame. The distinction between blame and accountability helped me finally let go of the anger and you may find that distinction helpful to you too. So let's explore this a little deeper.

You can hold someone accountable without feeding the anger inside you. When you hold someone accountable, you are able to see your own role in what has happened. You see the choices you made and the feelings and reactions you are having, and you hold yourself accountable for your part. You are also able to recognize their role in what occurred. Inasmuch as you are willing to hold yourself accountable for your actions and your choices, you create an opportunity for others to be accountable as well. Accountability includes a willingness to make amends, understand the perspective of the other person, and have compassion for yourself and the other person for making a less than optimal choice.

Blame, on the other hand, leads to an angry, energetic punishment of others and ourselves. When you punish someone else in anger, you are likely to suffer as well—in guilt and frustration at the very least. Other people frequently get roped in to the cycle of energetic punishment—those you want to punish and other people around you who bear the burden of your actions.

Let's clarify this concept with a family situation. Let's say you are one of three children in a family. All of you have moved away from home and live on your own. You and your siblings each have a child. Your parents absolutely adore their grandchildren. Your brother makes a serious choice that embarrasses your parents and makes them angry. Your father blames your brother for bringing shame to the family, so your father decides to disown his son. Now your brother, along with your entire family, must live with the results of that blame and punishment. Your parents don't get to see one of their beloved grandchildren, nor do the grandchildren get to see their cousins very often because your brother does not get to join you for family gatherings, and you and your other sibling are living in the heart-breaking dynamics of a family torn apart.

Your father gets to believe he is right and made a righteous choice—at the expense of the entire family. Everyone lives with the stress and punishment seemingly inflicted on one person. If the father's desired result is healing, balance, respect or any other positive family quality, the atmosphere of blame chokes off any hope of respect and a positive family dynamic. It is far more likely to create a spiral of blame, with the ostracized brother blaming the father, the mother and siblings blaming one or more family members, and on and on into an abysmal pit of negative feelings.

Remember, blaming someone else for the discomfort you feel emotionally or physically is not a solution if you are intent on healing, even if that someone played a significant role. Let's look at this family again. Maybe the brother did do something his father was shamed by. Let's say the son took a job with his father's business competitor. His action could be difficult to accept, but he is not responsible for his father's feelings. The son is responsible for his actions, but his father is responsible for his own feelings and his response to his son.

His father could have chosen to respond to his son with a heart-to-heart talk explaining how he felt. The father might have asked his son why he made that decision and really listened to the answer in order to understand his son better. The father could have expressed his disappointment and asked his son to reconsider his course of action, even requesting his son make a choice that demonstrated more care and concern for his family. In the end, however, his son must make his own decisions for his life, and the father must make the decisions for his own life. If the son chooses to keep his job with the competitor, the father will probably feel something—maybe betrayal, hurt, sadness, frustration or anger. The father's feelings are his own responsibility to understand, process and heal—not his son's. To expect his son to change so that the father will feel better sets up an opportunity for resentment, not healing. If healing the wound or gap between them is important, it will happen through love, compassion and a desire to understand the other, not through blame and punishment. As you can see, the blame loop doesn't allow much room for understanding to occur. So if healing is a serious desire, it begins with self-responsibility.

The same is true when you are blaming and punishing yourself for something you have done, believed, experienced, or at some level allowed, that you are ashamed about. In the case of emotional and physical illness, you can be punishing yourself and not even realize it. Self-debasement can be very insidious. You can be beating yourself up emotionally and physically, projecting it on to the people around you so that it looks like the problem is with them, yet all the while, deep inside, you are more upset with yourself than you are with anyone else in your life. The way out of the loop is in taking responsibility here and now for what you truly have the most influence over—you.

Finding ways to understand all the choices you have made, including the ones you are ashamed of, is a significant step to take in promoting your healing. Guilt is a nasty energy that can bind you in pain for years. Some years ago I participated in a very powerful women's healing circle. A few of the older women courageously admitted to the circle they had abused their children when they were young. They did not go into details about the nature of the abuse; though their hearts spilled out the shame they had been carrying most of their lives. As I looked into the faces of these women, I recognized how much pain their faces held. All of the women had significant health issues and most of them smoked cigarettes. I remember thinking at the time that they were punishing themselves emotionally and physically, probably far beyond any punishment their own children would have chosen to balance the scales.

I felt deep compassion for these women and the tremendous pain they must have been carrying themselves that would cause them to abuse another. And then of course there was the ongoing pain of their guilt and shame. I saw only one cure—compassion. In that moment, I found a deep compassion for the lineage of men and women I came from. I recognized that pain begets pain until we stop it with compassion. I left the circle with a commitment to find understanding and compassion for the choices I regret, so that I would be able to take love with me, rather than guilt, when I die and make my crossing to the other side.

SEEING YOURSELF AS THE CREATOR OF YOUR REALITY

When you learn the art of releasing blame, you may find yourself embracing your journey more fully by taking more responsibility for the life you are creating. Though challenging at times, taking responsibility is rewarding. Your physical health, mental health, and even your relationships will all benefit as you become an observer of you, your choices, and your responses. You will recognize how much influence you really do have over your own well-being, not by trying to control or influence others, but by being truthful and supportive of your deepest needs and desires.

I had a crystal-clear example of this recently during an incident at my home. My husband and I were out snow blowing and shoveling some heavy snow off of our very long driveway. Because the snow was heavier than usual, I was getting tired and my muscles were aching more than usual. I was ready to quit, when my husband asked me if I had shoveled out the hot tub (my usual job). I almost told him my back was aching too much to do any more, but acknowledging a hot soak would feel exceptionally good, I went around back and started digging out the tub.

Since my husband was almost finished with the driveway, I assumed he would come around back and give me a hand in a few minutes. As time went on I wondered where he was, and my mood was getting progressively worse as my back continued to complain. I was on the last few shovel-fulls when my husband opened the back door. With a puzzled look, he told me he thought I would have been finished by now. I snapped at him that the snow was heavy, my back ached and this was taking much longer than usual. I also informed him I assumed he would have come around to help me. In anger, I thrust my shovel into the snow for another load and threw my back out.

Now, my back had been aching up until that moment, but I wasn't necessarily in danger of throwing it out. In my anger, I didn't move cautiously. I thrust the shovel without being careful and threw my back out of alignment. It was my angry reaction that created the injury. I resented my husband for abandoning me. But even worse, at the real core of my frustration I realized I was angry with myself for being angry with him. I knew better than to make assumptions, and I had assumed he would come help me, and then I had assumed he had abandoned me to hard labor in the back yard. I could have asked for help. I could have told him I was too sore to shovel out the hot tub. I could have stopped at any point and made a positive choice on my own behalf, but instead I allowed myself to blame him, and in the end I realized I was angry for letting myself resent him.

Fortunately my husband is a great guy. He immediately got me into the house, apologized for not realizing I could have used his help and made sure I got into a comfortable chair. In the presence of his kindness, I actually felt worse because then I felt guilty for being angry with him. Sitting still with a heating pad gave me plenty of time to reflect on what had happened. As I have stated, the emotional content I believe triggered me was anger with myself for being angry with my husband, and my anger was exacerbated by a complex mixture of additional feelings including a desire to be right, wanting to be vindicated, and wanting to receive sympathy. Subconsciously, I wanted sympathy and throwing my back out was a way to make him feel guilty enough to be sympathetic. I was trying to punish him as well as myself and so I subconsciously, and somewhat consciously, created an injury to do it. Self-punishment can be so sneaky because it can be buried in all sorts of emotions, yet there it was. I was punishing my husband and myself.

By becoming a neutral observer in the midst of my emotions, I was able to witness the confluence of feelings and motivations that resulted in me injuring my back. If I had continued blaming my husband, I would have found myself retreating into resentment and anger that would have likely resulted in making derogatory comments directed toward him. Since the motivation for him to feel guilty and for me to receive sympathy would still have been at play, it is likely, in my need to feed my desire for sympathy, it would have taken quite a while for my injury to heal, or worse, I might have subconsciously created yet more injuries. There was only one way out and that was to recognize and release myself from the blaming cycle, applying the best healing balm—compassion.

Once I realized this, I was able to remind myself to be kind to myself. I apologized to my husband for blaming him when I was the one who needed to take better care of myself. Now I could have then blamed myself for blaming him, which would have simply perpetuated a spiral of negative thoughts and feelings. Instead, I chose to laugh at my stubbornness, receive the lesson about listening to my body's complaints, and remind myself in the future to respond early and proactively to my body's needs. I scheduled a massage and for the next week, gently coaxed my aching body back to health.

WHEN NOT TO TAKE RESPONSIBILITY

As we have discussed, we limit our healing potential when we make someone else fully responsible for what is happening in our lives, and do not recognize our own responsibility. Another way in which we limit our healing potential is when we assume responsibility for more than what is our responsibility. For example, if my parents did not heal from cancer, and I develop cancer, I could easily assume from what I witnessed in their process that I am doomed. Regardless of what treatment I am utilizing, if in my heart I perceive none of it will do any good, it probably won't. If I thought I had anything to do with or could have done something to prevent my parents' suffering and death, my guilt would only add to my sense of hopelessness as I assume responsibility for their suffering and my own. It is one thing to witness another's suffering and feel compassion for them and quite another to make their illness, doubts or fears our own.

By assuming responsibility inappropriately you might also affect someone else's healing. This is particularly true if as a healer or health professional you take responsibility for other people's successes. This became quite apparent to me when a friend of mine had a biopsy done on some tissue in one of her breasts. Since the tumor was benign and my friend is an energy healer, she decided she wanted to use some natural energy treatments before subjecting herself to surgical removal. She intended to schedule a second biopsy within six months to monitor her progress, recognizing she would be willing to have the lumpectomy if her methods were unsuccessful.

When the second biopsy was done the doctor's report mentioned nothing about the size of the tumor having been reduced significantly upon the second examination, admittedly by my friend's use of alternative healing methodologies. The doctor was able to remove the remainder of the lump; however, the report did not indicate anything had happened to the tumor between the first biopsy and the second. No one reading these reports would ever get the impression that the alternative methods my friend was using were actually having any effect. The reader of the report is left with the assumption that conventional medical treatment was the only effective treatment used. Thus, a non-invasive, gentle and effective healing technique that could have been considered as a potentially viable treatment is rendered nonexistent by what the report implies.

In this case, because it was not reported accurately, knowledge about the range of effective treatments for this condition became limited. If this occurred every time someone successfully used energy medicine, medical science would not have accurate data about the methodologies used to treat the condition, thereby potentially limiting the options of patients looking for less-invasive means of addressing similar conditions.

Knowing what responsibility to take and what not to take is a matter of spiritual ethics. If I acknowledge a healing journey as a spiritual journey, then I need to consider the ethical standard I choose to uphold in that journey. Personally, I find greater happiness when I assume 100% responsibility for the life I am living. I experience more satisfaction in life when I'm not adopting someone else's challenges or stealing from someone else's success—and that is taking full responsibility for the reality I am creating. When I take responsibility it means I am willing to heal the root cause, and any subconscious needs being met, in order to create a new reality for myself.

PAIN CAN BE ADDICTIVE

There is an ironic sweetness in pain. The sweetness I am describing is the subconscious need that is being fulfilled. It could even be described as the addictive nature of pain, injury and illness. This occurs when a subconscious need is being met through the suffering. For me there is a perceived esteem that comes with being righteous—with being the martyr. These are moments where the subtext behind my actions is, "Look at all that I am doing for you, and that is all you can do in return?" The problem with righteousness is it feels good, and that is what makes it so addictive.

With my back injury, unconscious needs were getting met. In order to understand the need, I simply asked myself in my quiet time with the heating pad, "What need is being met by injuring my back?" When I sincerely asked the question and stuck with it (uncomfortable as it was) until I got the answer, I discovered the confluence of motivations I described earlier. The addictive, unhealthy sweetness was exposed. I wanted my husband's sympathy because I wanted to be right, even at the expense of his feelings and my own health.

Because I am aware of this addictive dynamic, and once I observed what I was doing, I did not allow the urge to feed my need for sympathy, nor let my righteousness manipulate my husband into feeling guilty to motivate me any longer. I consciously made the choice to feel compassion for my husband and myself. As soon as I made the shift in my feelings, I was able to transform my anger into kindness. Only then was I able to truly embrace healing my injury. The moment I allowed compassion to permeate my feelings, I was open and ready to allow complete healing to occur. Hot packs, cold packs, rest, massage and sound healing worked quickly and efficiently to bring me physical strength once again. The treatments became appropriate expressions of loving sympathy that could truly fulfill me. I got to be right about knowing myself and acting on my own behalf, rather than being right about what I thought my husband should do. I also dug down deep inside myself to find compassion for the way I once again attempted to get my needs met by assuming rather than simply asking for what I needed.

By meeting my needs in healthier ways, I actually experience more fulfillment than I do through more addictive channels. While I have to admit righteousness gives a kind of immediate high, it doesn't fill my soul long term the way compassion satisfies me. Righteousness and its counterpart, judgment, have to be fed regularly; otherwise I start feeling depressed. But compassion—one good dose—and I feel great for a very long time.

REFRAINING FROM MAKING ASSUMPTIONS

As I have shared, one of my family patterns is to make assumptions, with my favorite assumption being that I am always right. As I work with others, I have come to realize it is a pattern fairly common in many families. It seems to be so pervasive that the Toltec mystery school has one of four agreements for freeing belief systems that is completely dedicated to not making assumptions. Don Miguel Ruiz, in his *The Four Agreements Companion Book"* says this about making assumptions: "We have the tendency to make assumptions about everything. The problem with making assumptions is that we believe they are the truth. We make an assumption, we misunderstand, we take it personally, and we end up creating a whole big drama for nothing."

This premise is so important to the teachings of the Toltec that Ruiz holds the agreement of not making assumptions above the other three agreements when he says: "With just this one agreement, you can completely transform your life."

As Ruiz points out, assumptions create dramas as they certainly did in my life. Dramas took a lot of energy, made me feel depressed and angry, and severely limited my perception of reality as well as my ability to find common ground or compassion with others. In the process of surrendering my assumptions, I discovered my healing gift with sound medicine; my dreams and meditations started showing me greater perspectives about the universe, spiritual realms and human existence; I developed more friends because I wasn't so busy judging them; and I learned to fall in love with what I didn't know. The unknown became a place of adventure rather than a place to fear. My life began unfolding like a rose in full bloom. Life became sweeter because I was living in the moment in its true nature instead of creating a drama around it.

One of my class participants made a very astute observation about one of her life-long assumptions. She realized that a very old assumption she had lived with most of her life was based on an experience in which she was wounded deeply. As a result, she drew a conclusion about how life was for her and lived out her life based on that negative assumption. The depressing feelings behind the assumption were oppressive, and the feeling was driving her life. As she began to test the assumption, she discovered there were many ways she could choose to believe, and many perspectives to consider. With time and meditation, she released the old assumption and opened to a greater healing perspective that brought her both healing and joy.

Another participant in one of my classes echoed this by sharing her life-long perception that life was hard. Here again, the feelings that accompanied this perception were powerful and overwhelming. Learning how to release this assumption, and even more importantly, the compelling feelings associated with the assumption became an incredible journey of self-discovery and eventually—emotional freedom. Instead of assuming healing had to be difficult, she opened to the idea that healing could actually be an enjoyable process. Imagine the difference such a perception could make in your healing journey. Instead of living with a limiting perspective that is difficult to bear, you could decide to open to a greater potential within you.

When I first started seeing doctors about what turned out to be a severe hormone imbalance, some of the doctors told me my condition was apparently normal for me and there was nothing that could be done about it. If I had believed that completely, I probably would not have been open to my friend's suggestion to see her endocrinologist. If I had continued feeding the drama I had with my mother, we would never have experienced that beautiful, transformative moment of her healing. If I had believed my assumptions when I threw out my back shoveling snow, I would have experienced a slow recovery and a strained relationship with my husband. I might never have explored sound healing or any form of energetic healing because I would have assumed it was crock and didn't work. Assumption might have led me to the conclusion it wasn't proven, so it couldn't be real.

Making assumptions can limit your healing. A friend of mine had a serious knee injury when he was younger and was told he would never walk again. He not only walks freely today, he continues his development as a martial artist. If he had assumed the doctor was right, he would likely be in a wheel chair today. You probably know someone who was told something similar to this and beat the odds. It makes me uncomfortable when someone I know is told by a professional they only have a certain amount of time to live or they won't ever be able to do something again. Even when they are based on convincing statistics, statements like this are assumptions that can hinder someone's Divine will and creativity. And if we believe statements like these, we are choosing to accept those limits. Then we create the limited drama that has been suggested instead of embracing our creative life force to manifest the life we desire.

Remember my friend who called me regarding her mother's surgery? She was worried about her mother going in for surgery to have a hernia removed. I assumed she was calling because she was worried. If I had not made that assumption, I would have listened more carefully to the subtext behind her words. I would have asked her questions about her concern that could have led to further investigation about the doctor. Intuitive impulses can be subtle. Making assumptions, in this circumstance, clouded my ability to recognize her intuitive voice.

When I was a school teacher I was familiar with studies demonstrating that students achieve to the level of expectation their teacher has of them. In other words, if I expected my students would achieve little, they would meet my expectation. If I expected they could meet significant goals, they did. I actually saw this in action when I was hired to teach a class of severely disabled children. In looking at their individual education programs over the course of several years, they once had a teacher who held high expectations and the children met their goals. The year before I was hired, they had a teacher who felt so badly for their disabled state, she set very low goals and the children only performed to that level. When I began teaching, I set high yet realistic goals for them to achieve. The children met their goals, and in riding the energy of their successes, sometimes exceeded the goals I had established.

In healing, I set high goals for myself and then put my full attention on meeting those goals. I ask people I love and trust to hold my vision with me. If they are inclined to pray for me, I let them know what prayer I am holding for myself so their thoughts and intentions can support mine. I surrender my healing to Divine will so the outcome will be what is truly best for me, including that which my mind has not fathomed yet. Like my students, I frequently exceed my goals. And if my healing has setbacks, then I know I probably need to break my goals into smaller steps so that I can become successful and continue building on my successes. I question the root cause of the illness, the reason I am experiencing a setback, and open to the answers (from wherever they may come) that will set me free from the limited conditions of my illness. By taking responsibility and simultaneously releasing assumptions about if I can heal or how it is supposed to happen, I am able to open my heart and mind to the Divine guidance that leads me to my healing.

WHAT IF YOU DISCOVERED YOU CHOSE YOUR LIFE?

Someone once posed a couple of intriguing questions to me that got me to look at my entire life in a whole new way. The questions were, "What if you had some say before you got to Earth about who your family would be? How would that influence your view about your childhood and your life?"

My first thought was, "No way. I didn't choose this dysfunctional life." But those are the kind of questions that haunt you until you at least try them on for size. Otherwise, given my beliefs at the time, I was going to have to assume God was either cruel or crazy. Or perhaps my soul was hanging out in some far-out bar and I had just smoked some very wild stuff, when a recruiter came around asking for volunteers for tough Earth assignments. The only other possibility I could imagine was that God, me, or both of us believed I could transform a stressful childhood into an adulthood for some greater good I couldn't quite imagine yet, and if that was true, I had to understand what greater good I was here to do. If I did choose this life, I must have had a worthwhile reason and I wondered what the heck that might be.

So, I imagined my soul was existing in some comfortable setting and I was writing my case argument for life on Earth. I explained why I was choosing these parents, at this time period, in this city. I argued for my parents' political persuasion, cultural backgrounds, religious views, income level, social perspectives, personal challenges and personal strengths. I then listed gifts I would bring with me, such as talents, intellect and aptitudes to help me in my journey on Earth. I explained how I would use the adversities and gifts of this childhood to learn, develop compassion and eventually evolve into a better human being.

When I finished, I was in shock! I no longer had a single reason for blaming my parents for any of their inadequacies as humans or as parents. I didn't have a reason to blame God either, or myself. All I had left was the naked realization of my ability to take a difficult, painful beginning and use it to turn myself into a realized human being. If I did choose my life, I had come prepared with all the gifts and talents I could possibly need to turn a challenging life into one of great meaning and fulfillment. I was completely responsible for every aspect of my life.

I don't know that I ever actually wrote out a case argument before coming to Earth, but after doing this exercise, I opened to the possibility that I had some say in who I was going to be before I ever incarnated in human form. I am willing to accept I probably chose my path before I got here, because if I knew the probabilities of this life and chose it anyway, my life makes greater sense to me.

I also feel a greater sense of self-empowerment, knowing that every time I transform pain into joy, I am one more person shifting the consciousness of pain as an assumed reality on this planet. I am consciously changing an assumption that, "There is pain and there is nothing I can do about it," to one of, "There is pain and I can transcend it." I have experienced pain in order to learn how to become free from pain. And with each day I experience less pain and greater joy because I continue to learn how to transform pain into freedom.

The concepts of pain being an assumed reality and that you can transcend pain to experience freedom may be a little difficult to grasp. Firewalking was the experience that helped me understand this. Yes, that is right, walking on fiery, hot coals….and in bare feet. The first time I went to a firewalk, I gave myself complete permission to not walk. This was very important because I was able to attend the workshop without any pressure from myself to walk on extremely hot coals. I decided ahead of time to walk only if that was the absolute right choice for me to make.

There I was standing at the fire, watching people walk across red-hot coals barefoot. They weren't getting burned! And somehow, that seemed normal to me. I don't think I could explain the reason it seemed normal, but I was accepting it as normal. Before the end of the firewalk, I was at the head of the fire, with no pressure from me or anyone else, just a deep desire to walk across those coals, and I did. When I got to the other side, I had no burns, no pain. I felt happy, blissful and free.

I was an ordinary woman who had shed my long-held belief that hot things burn you and then you feel pain. It wasn't logical to me, but it was a real experience. Just to make sure it wasn't a strange and unique mystical experience, I went to several more firewalks and came away with my tender feet in perfectly healthy condition. Now, if the idea of firewalking is intriguing to you, I do recommend you do it with an experienced instructor to help ensure your safety. People can and do get burned, but very few, and I have rarely seen it happen. However, I have always attended firewalks with competent instructors I trust.

During the firewalks, I experienced what I would describe as a transcendent state where the belief about fire and getting burned was lifted. It was not in my conscious belief. I successfully walked on coals unharmed and without subsequent pain from a burn. I learned there are states of consciousness that can lift us from limited beliefs about our assumed reality. That's right, assumed. We assume we will burn and so we do. But in this environment, I held no assumption about becoming burned and didn't. I assumed I would walk safely and did.

I can barely describe the feeling of freedom that filled me to my core in these experiences. It is more than freedom from pain. It is freedom from limiting beliefs and experiences. If I am in pain, I know I can take a pain reliever to reduce the pain and therefore experience freedom from pain. But that is not the same as just plain freedom. Freedom occurs when you know you are not bound by previously limiting beliefs. Can you imagine how the firewalking experience opened my perceptions about the human capability to transcend suffering and pain? If I could overcome such a well-accepted concept like "fire burns," what else could I transcend?

Some years later a friend reported to me he was able to cut off feelings of physical pain. I had been working with energy healing a long time and this was the first time someone suggested you could just choose not to feel it. He shared with me a story about using an automatic nailer and accidentally nailing his foot. He said, "I cut off any feeling to my foot, so I didn't feel any pain while the nail was being removed and bandaged." I have tried this with little success, but my friend is credible, and after my firewalking experience I know that sometimes seemingly impossible experiences can happen. So I continue to practice greater energetic control over how much pain I am willing to experience.

I have been testing this theory whenever I am not paying attention and do something like grab a hot item such as an oven rack. I don't panic. I don't react as though I have been burned. I don't put my hand in ice water or rub a salve on it, or put a protective bandage over it. I don't acknowledge a burn and I don't acknowledge pain. I tell myself it is just a kiss from the heat. My fingers do feel hot and ache; however, I seem to be able to recover from any discomfort within minutes to an hour. Even though this seems to be working for me with burns, I do not ignore all pain. I believe pain is an important message that something needs attention. However, as a result of my conscious work with burns, I am becoming more and more of a believer that pain management is within the reach of the human mind.

The more I see my life as a life of my choosing, the more I am able to consider that I can choose to live beyond commonly held beliefs. Initially, the concept that I had chosen my life with all its pain and suffering was unfathomable, but as I opened to the freedom of possibilities this concept allows, the more I found myself experiencing what others might call miracles. It caused me to wonder—if I did have influence over my own life; if I did have choices about how I would experience my life; if I could break through my preconceived limits— what miracles could I create?

LOOKING FOR MIRACLES

As we discussed earlier, one of the mistakes commonly made in the healing process is looking for a miracle. More than once, someone has come to me hoping my sound healing would cure them on the spot. This is easy to understand when someone has a life threatening or chronic illness. Of course they want to be done with it right now.

Because of the instantaneous healing I experienced with my mother in the hospital, for years, I also expected instant healing for myself and others, only to be disappointed when I discovered the healing process was going to take some time. Eventually, I realized my ego wanted the healing to happen immediately. Once I let go of the belief that healing had to happen in an instant, I made much better healing progress with myself and with my clients.

What has become apparent to me after singing healing songs to many people is that most illnesses have developed over several years. Sometimes those illnesses have been fed for a long time by fears of resentment, anger, self-loathing and despair. In many cases the likelihood of instant healing is minimal because the emotions need to be attended to in order for lasting healing to occur. Even if we did heal the physical illness in one session, the likelihood of that illness recurring or another illness taking its place is very high because the underlying emotional stressors and core beliefs that accompany the illness have not been healed.

Krystalya Marié, author of the *One Minute Energy Tune-Up, Power Symbols for Balanced Energy* says this about getting to core beliefs: "I cannot stress enough how important it is to get to the core belief and remove it before doing the belief transformation process with your new belief. If any of the old belief is still around, you will continue to repeat old patterns indefinitely until you finally identify the deepest non-supportive belief around the issue."

Healing that seems to be instant is usually happening because the person being healed has been addressing the issues, particularly the most core issue, behind the illness for some time. The willingness to face the doubts and fears behind the illness, understand their purpose for existing, and embrace new and more positive beliefs, culminates in a sense of immense freedom and receptivity that opens a doorway for powerful, and seemingly instantaneous, healing to occur.

Healing can happen very quickly when you are in a completely receptive and trusting state of mind and heart. I believe that is why my mother responded to my healing song so quickly. After our heart-to-heart talk, she seemed to be at great peace with herself. I know my heart was wide open and I imagine the same was true for her. That was probably all that was needed for her to open to healing. Though the actual moment of healing occurred in minutes, I also know it took my mother and I at least two years of personal work to be ready for that single moment of compassion and ultimate healing.

Instant healing, without the accompanying emotional work or

physical effort, is also easy to doubt. You might wonder if the healing is real because it happened so quickly and with so little effort. Doubt, like fear, allows your hopes to become swallowed up. As long as any doubt remains in your consciousness, you will ultimately keep yourself bound in a state of unwellness. So releasing doubts and fears fully and completely, for many people, is a journey that takes some time, practice and attention.

This concept became very clear to me some years ago. I had cut my finger quite deeply–almost deep enough to require stitches. I opted to use my sound healing to mend the cut, so I sat down, held my finger lovingly and began singing. My eyes were closed as I focused on seeing the cut completely healed as I sang the sounds coming to me intuitively. Finally, I opened my eyes to see how it was progressing. I audibly gasped as I saw the cut was almost completely sealed. Excited, I continued singing with my eyes closed, but when I opened them again, I had made no further progress on sealing the wound.

When I saw my energy medicine teacher a few days later, I told her what had happened. I asked her why the healing stopped after I had looked at the cut. She explained to me that my gasp was a statement of surprise and in this case the surprise was disbelief or doubt. She further explained that healing is normal. It should not surprise me. Because somewhere deep inside me I doubted, my body no longer responded to my sounds.

Over the years, I have discovered the single most significant factor in effective healing is to release doubts and focus my life force on the vision of healing wellness I am creating. Another energy teacher once suggested this to me, "See if you can hold your sound and vision of healing for 10 seconds without a break in your belief."

I thought, "Wow, is this going to be easy!" Silly me. That was the most challenging 10 seconds of my life, followed by the next most challenging 10 seconds of my life. My monkey mind found that 10 seconds is a long time to hold clear, exacting focus and heart-felt intention. Creating wellness takes focus—sustained focus—and that takes practice.

RECEPTIVITY

Another requirement of healing, often requiring adequate preparation, is receptivity—the kind of receptive state I described with my mother. Her entire being—heart, mind, body and soul—were ready and open for healing love. She didn't get there in an instant. That totally receptive state of grace took her months of preparation. When I am singing to someone who has opened fully, I can feel energetically when they have completely received what they needed. It feels like the tumbler of a lock turning and dropping into place. The person is unlocked and a new door in their life is opening. After years of observation about this, the degree of receptivity on the part of my client seems to make the difference between no effect for an unreceptive person to full effect for a receptive person.

Rather than looking for miracles, opening to guidance creates a much greater opportunity for the Divine to work through you. When you ask for guidance, you are more likely to receive information about the changes you need to make or the steps you need to take to progress your healing. If it is time for a leap, the acceleration in belief and faith required will be equally apparent to you if you are willing to receive guidance. It is much easier to miss the opportunity when you are looking for a grand miracle, but instead you are actually being given a step progressing you toward that miracle moment of healing.

IF YOU ARE AN EMPATH

If you are an empath, you have a unique challenge because you are extremely receptive. You experience other people's suffering, and some of you experience the turmoil of the planet itself, as if they are your own. You might be assuming all the chaos you feel is yours and therefore, something must be wrong with you because no matter what you do there is always more chaos and turmoil to heal. Or you may find it difficult to discern whether what you are feeling is truly yours or belongs to someone else.

Empaths I have known usually discover in the course of their healing journey that they have a particularly strong energetic healing talent to assist them in processing energy. You may find the best place to begin your healing process is with yourself and your own beliefs and feelings. By using your natural healing talent to help you transform your distressing, painful energy into love and compassion, you will have begun the process of getting some relief. You are probably also someone who needs to use energetic healing to cleanse yourself and rejuvenate yourself every day. By tending to your energetic healing diligently, you process negative thought forms and beliefs within you and attached to you, re-creating them into loving energy. Also, you will probably find that regular meditation helps you maintain a sense of perspective and balance regarding yourself and the world you live in.

As you engage this daily energetic cleansing and transformation process, you will probably find yourself naturally processing your own doubts, fears and concerns, transforming them into peaceful, loving perspective. You may find yourself identifying with deeply imbedded universal fears among humans such as abandonment, unworthiness and fear of the unknown. As these feelings come up, whether or not they feel as though they belong to you, you have the wonderful ability to transform them through your compassion. Because you are so sensitive to the universal energies, attention to your daily practice is vital to your health.

Since we are all connected through the Divine, what you attend to in your daily meditations and energy healing processes allows energy to transform both personally and universally. Feelings typically transform as soon as they are fully witnessed. If you are angry, you are likely to remain angry until you truly understand your anger. When finally fully witnessed, anger dissipates and transforms into another feeling—often sorrow. When sorrow is fully witnessed, it dissipates and transforms— often into peace. Peace becomes happiness and happiness—joy. Joy—bliss. Though not always followed in this precise order, feelings do change from one to another, particularly when witnessed in their fullness.

Empaths often come with an exceptional ability to allow feelings to flow through you, and hopefully, transform them as needed in the process. You may discover you become seriously ill if you hang on to feelings of anger and sorrow because the flow of your natural energy is blocked. Because you can too easily make the feelings personal, you may become overwhelmed by negative feelings, eventually becoming physically sick. Diligence and nonattachment need to become your dear friends in order to keep yourself whole and healthy.

If you are an empath, you are not the kind of person who does well watching, listening to or reading the news. You probably internalize and personalize negative events happening around the world. You are not likely the best sounding board for your friends' problems because you internalize their struggles as your own too easily. Of course, you can't escape all the negativity around you, nor would you necessarily want to. One of your gifts for the planet is to process general negative energy and transform it, so a certain amount of awareness may even be helpful to you. However, steeping yourself in negative points of view about life is dangerous to your health. You need to find an acceptable point of balance that works for you, probably oriented to positive events more than negative ones.

I went through a time in my spiritual development when I was particularly empathic and sensitive to everything and everyone around me. My elder and teacher taught me to keep engaging in the world, not to cloister myself in my house, but to notice what was happening as I engaged people and new environments. She encouraged me to notice my body when I entered new space, thereby learning to discern feelings more closely linked to me and feelings more connected to others.

Here is what my elder taught me that you can try for yourself: Let's say you enter a room and before you entered your heart was feeling fine, but it started hurting as soon as you walked into the room, take note. If there is someone in the room you feel drawn to, find a way to appropriately and casually touch them on the arm or hand. If the pain goes away, you now know the issue causing the pain is not yours. It might be appropriate to offer a prayer for their healing because you are empathizing with it. If the pain remains, even if it is their own issue causing their pain, you have an issue as well. You need to address the cause of your own pain.

Sometimes an empath is connecting to the planet and what he or she is experiencing is a type of cry for help. A dear friend of mine used to get terrible migraine headaches without warning. We weren't able to trace them to stress, hormones or any of the usual culprits. Finally, I did a healing meditation with her and saw a volcano of energy blasting through her head. I asked intuitively if this was a metaphor for something going on in her life and got a clear, "No." Then I asked intuitively if she was processing energy for Mother Earth through her body. This time I heard a clear, "Yes."

When she starts feeling pressure in her head, my friend now knows to create some quiet time to be with Mother Earth, particularly any volcanoes getting ready to erupt, and to send loving energy to the Mother as she gets ready to release this pressure. Regular meditations with Mother Earth help tremendously as she honors her unique empathetic relationship with the Earth. To my knowledge, since she understood the source of those headaches and began meditating with the Mother, she no longer gets those regular migraines.

Empaths have the most challenging job of all when it comes to knowing what responsibility is yours and what belongs to someone else. Yet, you have a powerful and special gift for creating energetic balance, so daily attention to healing your core issues by witnessing your own feelings, and witnessing other people's pain or the planet's traumas without lingering attachment to the feelings will help you find greater pleasure and comfort in your life. Because we all share in some universal feelings, you can help yourself and others by simply witnessing the feeling without attachment. Your understanding and compassion will be healing balm for yourself and anyone else ready to find peace with the more tumultuous feelings. Remember, the other side of pain is bliss, so as you do your transformative work, you will be creating tremendous harmony for you, others and the planet.

DISCOVER HOW THE TRUTH REALLY DOES SET YOU FREE

Ask questions that test your assumptions in order to uncover deeper truths—the subconscious needs being met through the illness—so that you can meet those needs in new and healthier ways.

Imagine still living with the assumption that bathing in any kind of water could be a source for contacting the plague, as it was during the Dark ages? Imagine still believing that knowing how to use herbs for healing was a sign you were evil? Consider living with the assumption that if you can sense things before they happen you are crazy and need to be locked up? When you are afraid to ask questions—to really understand yourself and the people and world around you—your life is based in assumptions. As we discussed in the previous chapter, assumptions can be hazardous to your life and your health.

QUESTIONING YOUR ASSUMPTIONS

We improve our understanding about how life in our universe really works by asking questions and testing our assumptions. This premise is clearly understood in our pursuit of scientific knowledge. This premise is also applied when a young adult questions the assumptions of his or her parents as she or he engages the process of defining their own beliefs as an adult. We question our political decisions, our social responsibilities and our business decisions. Many people choose to research and then treat the source, not just the symptoms, of their physical pain. In many ways, we understand the need to question our reality, consider new possibilities, test our hypotheses and adapt to new perceptions based upon what we learn in our discovery process. Yet, there are four areas in which I find I was initially resistant and my clients are reticent to question assumptions. They are:

- The source of conditioned/inherited beliefs that could be limiting your ability to heal physical distress
- The source of the emotional beliefs that may be keeping you in anguish
- The source of knowledge-based beliefs that limit your perception of healing possibilities
- The source of spiritual beliefs that limit your view of Divine power

Resistance occurs because these areas of consideration require you take personal responsibility for the reality you are experiencing and creating. Once you begin asking questions in these areas of your life and stay with the process of inquiry, there is nowhere to hide from yourself. There is no organizational structure or entity or person outside of you who is responsible for what you have come to believe and accept as real for you. And perhaps the greatest reason for resistance is an underlying fear about the direction your life would take and the responsibilities you would have if you were completely physically, emotionally, and spiritually happy and free.

ASKING CHALLENGING QUESTIONS

Questioning your own beliefs takes a lot of work, courage, and often demands change in thought and behavior if you wish to create greater happiness in your life. And change is not always fun, so no wonder questioning these areas isn't very popular. However, questioning long-held beliefs and getting down to the core beliefs that keep you locked in familiar patterns that aren't working is where the rubber meets the road when it comes to healing.

It is so much easier to blame problems on someone else than it is to address the beliefs we have adopted for ourselves. For years, I blamed my parents for the physical and emotional turmoil I experienced on a daily basis. I was angry with them for the abuse I experienced as a child, the limiting beliefs they taught me to accept as ultimate truth, and the adult responsibilities I felt forced to accept as a young child. From my perspective for many years, I was abused and it was their fault.

It was easier to see the flaw in someone else's beliefs and behavior than it was to take a look at my own limiting beliefs. Because once I looked at myself, I realized those patterns were ingrained in me and I now abused others and myself in both overt and passive ways. Once I made the choice to ask myself some challenging questions, my healing and my happiness accelerated dramatically. I went from feeling helpless and ineffective to feeling empowered to create the reality I wanted and dreamed about.

So what is a challenging question? Challenging questions are the ones that require us to look at our own responsibility in the matter. For example, if I am experiencing physical pain that is not healing I might consider what I have been conditioned to believe over time by asking, "What benefit(s) do I get from being in pain?" A challenging question addressing emotional healing might be, "In what way do I blame someone else for my current emotional problems?" Another question I might ask would be "What feelings am I suppressing by over-analyzing my personal issues?" A challenging question regarding my knowledge base might be, "How am I limiting my healing options by overriding my intuition, or am I assuming intuition is not based in a form of knowledge?" Or I might ask, "What am I afraid to understand about this condition?" To address my spiritual beliefs, I might ask, "Do I truly believe God is punishing me through my physical illness, or is there some other dynamic at work?"

These are challenging questions to ask yourself, because now the onus is on you to better understand the challenges you have allowed to come into your life. The good news about asking challenging questions is that you seem to naturally want to follow up the answer to the challenging questions with yet another question leading you to resolution or what I call a free-will question. Here you might ask, "How could I get my core needs met through something other than physical pain?" Or, "What do I need to know or believe in order to experience ongoing emotional happiness?" For mental clarity I might ask, "What knowledge do I need to help me balance my intuitive feelings with insights from research in order to determine right action?" In regard to spirituality, you might consider, "What Divine insight will help me discover and experience lasting physical comfort?"

Notice not one of these questions asks what someone else could or should do to help me feel better. For example, asking myself if I blame someone else for my emotional state means I'm going to take a look at who I am holding responsible for my emotional well-being. If I am holding someone else responsible, it is not likely I am holding myself responsible. As a child, I saw my whole world as influencing my emotions and my life, but as an adult claiming my healing power, I choose to see how I have accepted someone else's influence as being more powerful than my own.

By choosing the state of emotional reality I want to experience and choosing to make changes in my beliefs and actions that promote my preferred emotional state, I recognize my power to create the reality of my desires. Because emotions and beliefs can drive physical experience, in affirming beliefs that promote ongoing happiness, I have opened my creative mind to a world of possibilities leading me to a greater state of well-being. The questions I ask become significant change agents in my journey of health. The responsibility is all mine, and that is where personal power lives. I realize my job is to ask myself my questions and make the changes where I have the most control and influence—with myself.

QUESTIONS THAT OPEN YOUR ENERGY

When you do ask your free-will questions, it is wise to consider questions that open your energy. You should feel uplifted by your question. Even if it makes you a little nervous, the question should inspire hope. Open-ended questions are best, such as "How can I....? What do I need to do or believe in order to......? Open-ended questions allow the Divine flowing through you to show you your pathway to health. By asking open-ended questions and then paying attention to your body and feelings you are opening to a greater experience of your intuition and the Divine wisdom within you.

If I ask a more limited question, I may find myself feeling depressed or hopeless. Such a question might be asking God, "Why am I being punished?" "What did I do to deserve this?" These questions make an assumption about the nature of God, and they are not very positive assumptions. Or you might ask yourself, "Why am I constantly sick?" "Why can't I seem to heal?" These questions feed the drama, rather than open a pathway to greater wisdom. By asking instead, positive, open-ended questions for help and guidance in my healing, I am more likely to get answers that will actually assist me in exercising my free-will desire for greater health.

ASKING BOTH THE CHALLENGING AND FREE-WILL QUESTIONS

If the free-will questions seem more alluring to you and you think you don't need the challenging questions, you might want to consider this course of action carefully before leaping over the challenging questions. The reason you may want to ask some challenging questions before you engage your free will is that you just might accept an easy answer that doesn't really get down to meeting your core need. If you get to the challenging questions first, you are more likely to identify the core need, and now when you engage your free will you will come up with creative means for meeting your core need. With practice you may discover you can indeed ask yourself the free-will oriented question only, and then by becoming still and really listening to your intuition, you will know the core need not being met, yet at the same time you understand what you can do to best meet that need.

I encourage you to give yourself permission to take steps in the beginning. Too often in spiritual healing practice I have watched myself and those I love attempt to by-pass the challenges to get to the good stuff. Most of us want the process to be easy. The process does become easier and easier, if in the beginning we have the courage to get to our absolute truth—the beautiful aspects of it and the not-so-beautiful aspects of our deepest truth. Skimming the surface of our truth, speaking about our core issues in broad generalities, addressing our issues from our minds and not from our feelings are all limits to greater consciousness. These are ways in which we avoid looking at how we might be causing harm to ourselves. The height of our true spiritual nature lives in the depths of who we really are, and our freedom lies in our courage to observe ourselves as we truly are—all of it. By seeing ourselves fully, in compassion, we are able to recognize the ways in which we may be meeting core needs through less-effective means; and therefore, make changes that allow those needs to be met through healthier choices.

Discovering the Underlying Needs Behind the Pain

A good friend once suggested to me that I consider a new concept regarding healing. He suggested the reason we remain in painful and difficult situations is because some core need is getting met. Once you identify the core need being met, you are able to consider new circumstances–healthier circumstances–through which that same need can be fulfilled.

Let's review the story where I describe my back going out when I got angry with my husband and continued shoveling snow in resentment. Here is a great example of more than one core need looking to be met in a less than healthy manner. I had a need to be right and a need for sympathy and I was looking to meet both of them by blaming my husband.

A more positive means for experiencing genuine, non-guilt-ridden sympathy might have been to tell my husband I was too tired to shovel out the hot tub at all, and stop when I was tired but still felt physically fine. I could have also gotten this need met in a positive way by simply asking my husband for his help. Or I could have simply stopped shoveling out the hot tub when my body was telling me to stop, gone into the house and in sympathy with my tired body–rested. By getting my need for sympathy met in a more positive manner, I wouldn't have injured myself and I would have had no need to try to make my husband feel guilty through my resentment, anger and back pain.

Remember, I also had a need to be right. Injuring myself made me right and my husband wrong. An unmet need to be right can quickly turn into righteousness and righteousness is at the root of oppression. Righteousness becomes, "I'm right and you are wrong." "I am better than you." "I know more than you." Whenever one person thinks they are better than another, they have created justification to oppress someone else. If you feel guilty about your belief or ensuing behavior, you can even end up oppressing yourself with self-debasement and illness. The way to be right, without making someone else wrong, or beating yourself up energetically is to act appropriately on your own behalf. In my case, I would have been *right* if I had listened to my body and stopped shoveling.

Needs are simply unfulfilled experiences. They are not bad or good. Needs exist whether we want them or not. If we didn't get much sympathy as a kid, we are very likely going to try to get that need met as an adult in whatever manner we can get the need met, whether or not it is a healthy means. So, if I ask myself the challenging question of, "What need is getting met through my illness or injury?" I can get down to the subconscious motivator(s) behind my unsatisfactory physical condition. Once I identify the need, I can give myself permission to fulfill the need in a healthier manner.

Identifying true core needs makes a difference when it comes to fulfilling needs. For example, if I'm having regular tension headaches, being headache-free certainly meets a need. However, if I am living a stress-filled life, what am I saying about the care and respect I have for myself? Am I placing money, prestige, career, other people's demands, or other matters over my own health? What does this say about respect for my body?

In this example, respect for my body may be the predominant core need requiring attention. To respect myself—my body—enough to change my lifestyle in order to be headache-free is more likely to meet my core need.

In watching myself and others stay with the difficult questions, I have noticed there is a breakthrough point when it comes to identifying core needs. If I am asked or ask myself a question to better understand my needs, and I flip off an answer to a question without really feeling what I am saying, I haven't gotten to the core need driving me yet. It is important to feel, and then speak. Best of all, if I stay with the question, feel what it brings up for me and speak from that place in an honest desire to understand my truth, tears usually start welling up. When the tears come forward, I'm there. I can feel the longing and have touched the core need that is yet unmet.

SELF-PUNISHMENT

When it comes to spiritual practice and healing it is easy to confuse self-punishment or self-sacrifice as God's punishment. As a child, I used to believe when good things were happening God was rewarding me and when bad things were happening God was punishing me. This belief makes sense as a child because that is what a child perceives his or her parents would do. However, this belief is spiritually limiting as an adult because it disregards one of our greatest recognized gifts as a human—free will.

Free will allows us to create our reality. If I embrace my free will and my opportunity to create my reality, I am accepting my Divine birthright to create the life of my choosing. Utilizing Divine will to create my reality, I might find great power in asking free-will questions to provide me with even more guidance and direction in my healing journey. I might ask, "What insight will free me from my pain?" Or perhaps, I would ask, "What gifts have I been given and how could I use them to free myself from physical pain?" Or "What other means would better meet my core needs, while ensuring my health?"

THE POWERFUL MOTIVATING FORCE OF EMOTION

Where we may find ourselves getting hung up is in experiencing the truth of our emotions. Because our emotions often motivate our actions and our beliefs, our emotions need our loving, attentive care. I commonly witness people trying to avoid their uncomfortable emotions, but bypassing them does not help us heal. In my experience, it limits us tremendously. In truth, our greatest healing work often lies in the emotions we fear the most.

A dear friend of mine once said to me, "The hardest spiritual work we do is in healing our emotional bodies. The most important work we will ever do is healing our emotional bodies."

Your fear of those emotions can become blocks in your healing because you aren't getting to what is motivating you at the core. You need to get to what is motivating you if you want to create significant and lasting positive change. You might be thinking, "But I don't know what to do when I come up against my fear." However, you probably do know how to address your fear if you think about a circumstance from your past in which you did it successfully. Many of us know how to transform our fear into awe-inspiring acts of creation. You simply need to apply the tools you have learned in life to addressing your emotions. Let's look at an example together that demonstrates how we as humans really do know how to work through our fear—one of the most powerful emotions.

If I am just learning how to play the piano, at first I am going to be learning basic fingering techniques and how to read music. Initially I might be overwhelmed. I might find it to be very challenging, even frustrating at times. I might be afraid I will never get the hang of this. Learning something complex can initially take every ounce of mental and physical skill, as well as enormous emotional energy. If I continue to practice, eventually my eyes will see the notes on the page and my fingers will respond to certain passages in what could practically be described as an automatic reflex. I see the music on the page and my fingers move. I move fluidly because I know the pathway. I know what the notes mean as cues and my fingers know what to do. Only when I am introduced to a brand new and more challenging piece of music will my fear and anxiety come up again, as I find myself needing to slow down to carefully learn each phrase.

With music I have learned, I am now able to focus on the interpretation of the piece rather than the technical nature of the music. Because the technique is in place, I am now ready to explore the subtleties of expression—making the piece a creative exploration of my free will. I focus on beauty, power, passion or whatever the piece needs to be a fulfilling creative experience.

The same process holds when I explore my emotions through questions. Initially, the questions are challenging and may even feel overwhelming. I might even want to shut down completely, or I might feel numb, confused or lost. By staying consciously with the question and the feelings that begin to come up, just like a new piano student staying with and practicing the musical phrase until it feels natural, eventually I will learn how to experience my feelings as being natural. With practice, I will be able to ask a question with both my heart and mind working together, searching deeply for the most significant response. As the technique becomes second nature, I discover the pathway to my core truth.

Once I know the pathway, I can now focus on my free-will expression. I can consider how to bring more fulfillment into the expression of my life. Just like an accomplished pianist, eventually technique becomes more automatic and I am able to focus on the actual experience and chosen expression of my feelings, knowing the mastery of my technique—my pathway to the truth—is now a part of me.

OVERRIDING INTUITION

I was a master at overriding my intuition. It was actually very easy to do. I would get a feeling about something, sometimes accompanied by one of those thoughts in the back of my mind about a direction or choice to make, and then I would logically make a case for taking a different course of action. Because I placed greater value in my logic than I did in my feelings, I persuaded myself to follow my logic. What I eventually discovered was that my intuition was usually more accurate than my logic when it came to my personal journey.

Here is an illustration about how I could override my intuition. I was getting in my truck to go pick up the medicine woman I was studying with at the time to take her to an appointment. As I started to get in the truck, it occurred to me I had better check the oil. I did and sure enough the oil was low. There was a store just blocks from where I lived that had the right oil for my truck, so I started up my vehicle thinking I would just pop over and pick up a couple quarts before heading to my teacher's house.

Something inside me kept thinking, "There is a store over by your teacher's house."

"Yes," I argued with myself, "but I want to get this done now."

If I had stopped to feel, I would have realized there was a feeling associated with this niggling thought in the back of my mind that I should wait until I got across town closer to my teacher's house. There was a slight anxiety about picking up the oil first. As I said, I was good at listening to logic, and my logic was that if I got the oil now, I wouldn't be likely to forget when I got across town. So I headed over to the nearby store, picked up the oil and took care of my truck. It was very good logic, but it turned out to be a less-than-optimal choice.

When I got on the freeway, a semi-truck had flipped over on its side and was blocking the entire set of lanes. I didn't have a cell phone back then, traffic was backed up for miles, and I was now going to be very late getting to my teacher's house, which meant I was going to be very late getting her to her appointment. All I had needed to do was ask myself a question, such as, "Why am I getting this thought to drive across town before putting oil in my truck?" Or I could have asked, "Should I be paying more attention to this thought in the back of my mind?" Questions like these would have opened up greater possibilities for information and the knowledge of my intuition. To better understand my intuitive wisdom, I could have considered how the two thoughts made me feel. Comparing the feeling of the thought, "Go to the store now," to "Go to the store later," would have given me some great insight. I would have realized my feelings were showing me the best course of action for me at that moment in my life.

Now, when I have conflicting thoughts, I ask myself, "How might my thoughts be reflecting my intuition?" Then I pause for a moment and search for clarity through the feelings in my body. If my body tightens up or I feel ill, the choice is not for me. If my body stays relaxed or feels good, the choice is a better one for me. Consistently, I find I am happiest with my intuitive choices.

By the way, intuitive feeling is not the same as emotional feelings— like being so head over heels with someone that I don't see the signs telling me this would not be a good relationship for me. I've seen people become afraid of their intuition because they confuse this kind of feeling with other emotions. In fact, in the situation I have just described, I might be feeling in love or in lust with someone, while overriding a sense that something is not quite right. Intuitive insight comes to you when you become quiet and still inside; when you settle your intense emotional feelings down, opening to your greatest inner truth—whether you like the truth or not—intuition at its best conveys your deeper truth.

SPEAKING YOUR TRUTH

I know when someone in one of my classes is really getting to their breakthrough to freedom, when they recognize and speak honestly about their limits. They aren't beating themselves up for their perceived limit, they are simply recognizing where they get stuck. Once seen, the limiting belief, fear or other emotion can now be addressed in a positive manner, and healing freedom is soon to follow.

The first person who needs to hear your truth is you. Beyond that, you may find it healing to share your truth with others. I have seen an interesting interpretation of sharing one's truth that I find disturbing and ineffective. Sharing your truth does not indicate license to beat up someone else with angry words and resentment. The feelings of anger may be true to how you are feeling, but things said in anger are often exaggerated, inflated versions of what is really the truth. Words spoken in cynicism and sarcasm come from a place of feeling less than adequate and unworthy. I used to be one of the most cynical and sarcastic people I knew. I made everyone else wrong so that I could feel adequate, and I was angry a lot of the time, so I easily justified my angry feelings by blaming everyone around me. My anger came from my feelings of inadequacy and inability to have any control over my life. That is where the truth was hiding. My anger was about me, not the world around me. Therefore, verbally attacking someone else was not helping me heal; it was feeding my anger and desire to blame someone else for my problems.

Speaking up for yourself contributes to your healing when you are stating your need to someone else, asking someone to support you in meeting your need in more positive ways, or asking someone to support you in making healthier choices. Speaking up is about defining the situation you find yourself in and want to change. You may find you need to muster some courage to speak your truth, if you are not used to doing so. In fact, you may find it very difficult to speak your truth without anger if you are not used to speaking up for yourself. However, you can learn to speak honestly without blame. As you do, you may be pleased to discover you have more allies in your healing journey than you realized. Invited warmly to help change an uncomfortable situation, others around you may be much more willing to join you in making new choices for a jointly healthier life style.

Being completely honest with yourself is a must. You can't fake yourself out when it comes to healing. I have seen people make statements about their healing that they want to believe are true, but aren't true yet, and limit their healing potential. This is tricky, because while you want to affirm the healing reality you are creating for yourself, if any part of you is saying in the back of your mind, "Yah, right!" you have a set up for self-sabotage. The simplest way to recognize when you are doing this is when you are saying, "Everything is fine," and everything is really *not* fine. Think of it this way—you just lied to yourself. Now, how can you trust yourself, when you lied to yourself? You can't. At least not all of your conscious and subconscious mind can trust you. At least one part of you, the part that feels lousy has evidence that you just say things to try to make you feel better—but really, you feel terrible. So the overwhelming evidence that you have now reinforced is that you feel bad. Trying to convince yourself that you feel better than you do is probably not going to get you the results you want.

So what do you do? Tell yourself the truth. You already know you hurt. You are not going to suddenly convince yourself you don't. Can you reduce the pain, turn it off or even heal so that there isn't any pain? Those are possibilities, and they are all within a realm of potential truth for you. If you are hurting, maybe it is time to engage your creativity, utilize a healing treatment, tap into your own healing energy. Is it time to meditate, sleep, see a doctor or healer, watch a funny movie, or focus your mind and feelings on wellness? Your discomfort may be telling you it is time to tend to yourself. Be truthful and honest about the pain you are feeling and then do what works for you to assist your healing process and minimize or eliminate your suffering. Then when you introduce a healing methodology or an affirmation you can truly believe in, all of your conscious and subconscious thoughts will be in alignment with your healing intention.

CHAPTER SIX — STEP SIX
LOVING THE WOUNDS
THAT CREATE THE PAIN

The greatest healing balm in the world is heartfelt compassion for yourself and others.

It took me a while, but I finally understood that forgiveness naturally happens when I have the courage to understand my motivation and the motivation of others with compassion. The day my healing journey really began was the day I finally stopped being so tough and so together, and allowed myself to feel heartfelt compassion for me. Up until that moment, I had been living most of my life from the motivations and perspectives of a wounded child, all the while pretending to be an adult.

The feelings of fear—abandonment, neglect, and not being understood or respected—had been driving my life, even though on the outside I was putting on a pretty good show that I was in control. From my naive perspective, everyone else was messed up, but I was fine, and only on rare occasion was I willing to take any responsibility for how my life was going. I was willing to assume I was responsible for my successes; but the challenges I faced, I preferred to assume were not my doing.

As we have explored, taking responsibility for everything that happens in your life is one of the steps to claiming your power and experiencing complete healing. Once you truly embrace your journey and take full responsibility for your life, it would feel pretty harsh to do so without compassion. After all, you have been a human being who for the most part has probably been doing your best. You have probably created some moments you are proud of and some moments that still bring you shame. In order to deal with the shame, you need to consider how your own wounded motivations may have been driving your feelings and choices. Once you acknowledge the wounded person who made the choices you are not proud of, you may find yourself able to feel compassion for yourself, thereby releasing the past and fully embracing your new state of realization, as well as compassion for others.

CLAIMING YOUR POWER

The essence of claiming your personal healing power lies in your ability to feel compassion for yourself. The cells of your body, along with your emotional memories carry the knowledge of your highs and lows as a human being. Emotional and physical pain often disappear with deep, caring self-compassion because someone has finally heard you, seen you, witnessed and understood you at your very core. No one can understand you as well as you can. So when it comes to compassion, you are your ultimate healer.

Consider what happens when you are having a fight with another person. You may find yourself struggling to be heard and understood by the person you are fighting with. As long as both of you remain focused on what each of you wants, the fight will continue because no one is really listening. However, if during this fight, the person you are arguing with stops and says, "Obviously neither of us is very happy and neither of us is feeling heard. I am going to go get a drink of water and when I come back I'm going to not say anything and just listen to you. I'm going to do my best to understand you even if I disagree." Then if the person listened with desire to understand, and even began to truly understand with compassion what you were saying, how would you feel?

Isn't it easy to imagine your shoulders relaxing and your voice softening as though the weight of the world was being lifted from you? And what if you could do that for someone else? Imagine someone you care about aching because they didn't feel heard. Imagine putting your own need to be heard on hold long enough to really listen to that person—to listen until you felt compassion. How would that person feel? How would you feel?

If either one of you created space for heartfelt listening, you would both begin to transform through that single expression of compassion. Those needs to be heard, seen, loved, respected, cared for, understood, and so on, often come from old, old wounds—times when our feelings were not cared about. We desperately want them to be met and as you know, we will even allow ourselves to become emotionally distressed, physically ill or injured in our attempts to get them met.

What is true in terms of your interaction with another human being is equally true when it comes to listening to yourself with your own heart. Once you listen to yourself with compassion and once the need is met, the need quiets down and you can move toward reconciliation. Understanding that the motivation behind the choices in your life comes from unmet needs, and then meeting those needs by attending to yourself with compassion, allows the healing process to truly take effect. You don't have to wait for someone else to do it.

Acting on your own behalf, compassionately understanding and giving yourself what you most need, without expectation from others, fills you from the inside out. Because you are filling yourself with respect, being heard, or any other quality that meets your core needs and heals old wounds, you will attract people into your life who embody the same qualities and treat you with the regard you long for. The moment you release expectations about others loving you and love yourself, you are claiming your power.

You can even claim your power if you are ill due to no perceived fault of your own. Let's say you have been exposed to airborne toxic chemicals from a nearby business. You breathe in the toxins and you become ill. You may not have known the business produced anything toxic you should be concerned about. You might be thinking, "I have a right to be angry with them. This isn't my fault. I don't have any responsibility in this and I certainly don't feel compassionate toward them."

It is appropriate to hold the business accountable for any harm they have perpetrated. However, remember that blame, anger and resentment only delay your healing. In order to further your physical and emotional healing, consider addressing your share of responsibility as well. This is a good time to ask yourself some of those hard questions. "Was my intuition alerting me before I moved into this area, and did I ignore it?" "Did I do all the research I could have done before choosing to live here?" "When I started feeling ill, did I do something about it right away?" "Did I seek proper medical and healing assistance immediately?" "Did I research other places to live as soon as I discovered the exposure?" "Have I asked for help from the government, community, friends and relatives to relocate myself to a healthier environment?" "Do I have the right mental and emotional presence to attract the healing help I need right now?" Consider that if you are feeling any guilt at all, you are probably feeling some responsibility, and taking ownership of your responsibility can set you free.

When you are feeling guilty, you might want someone to let you off the hook—to understand your motivation at the time of your choice and to forgive you for having been unable or unwilling to assume greater responsibility at that time. People all around you could tell you it is okay. They could tell you they understand, but deep down inside, the person you want to understand and forgive you is you. What truly heals you deep down inside is your own compassion. Therefore, even when at first glance it appears you had no responsibility, you might want to take a moment to see if you have any feelings of guilt.

Guilt, blame and accompanying resentment are the three feelings I consistently see inhibiting people's healing journeys. If you are feeling guilty, you may want to find some understanding and compassion for your choices. If you can feel compassion, you will be giving yourself a greater chance to relax, and in relaxing open more fully to the healing methodologies you are using. You will probably find a core need waiting to be met sitting behind the guilt, blame or resentments. You might discover an underlying need to listen more closely to your intuition or a desire to take more action on your own behalf.

As you give yourself permission to love the wounds within you and to fulfill your core unmet needs, you might find yourself desiring to expand your capacity to meet those needs. This is the moment when you are stepping out of the limits of illness and into the great spiritual adventure of healing. Consider helping yourself in this journey by asking yourself a free-will question such as, "What could I do to listen to myself better?" Or, "What would respecting myself look like?" Then watch and observe how the Divine mystery unfolds to you through new awareness and experiences.

THE HARDEST PERSON TO LOVE

The hardest person to love in my life has been me. I have also been the hardest person to forgive. My compassion wells up immediately for others, but when it comes to me I have been traditionally slower to empathy and understanding. The more I heal, the more that changes. Thank goodness. And the more I love myself, I have discovered, the greater capacity I have to love others more fully.

This realization became significantly apparent to me as I healed from the wounds of sexual abuse. When I first began the journey of remembering that I had been abused and was healing from the deep emotional scars of that trauma, I was resentful and blamed my abuser for being an awful person who robbed me of my innocence. As I progressed in my journey and chose to accept responsibility for my reality, I could no longer blame my abuser for the life I had chosen. Because I had accepted that I had some say in choosing this life and had agreed to live out this life complete with its traumas and its blessings, I could hold this person accountable for their actions, but I refused to blame my abuser as being solely responsible.

That meant I had to look at myself. In order to heal, I was going to have to forgive myself for choosing such a painful lesson. "How could I have chosen this?" I would ask myself. "Was I drunk? Or did I just make up this whole concept of self-responsibility? Maybe it is appropriate to blame someone for their poor choices! Or am I to blame?"

I raced back and forth between taking responsibility to shifting the blame back to my abuser. And when I was being hard on myself, I blamed myself. It was very scary for me to think I accepted and possibly attracted sexual abuse into my life in order to learn what I believed was a lesson about greater compassion. My spiritual journey had led me to the realization that my soul accepted abuse as part of my journey and drew it in to my earthly experience, and I was having a difficult time living with this.

Every time I stepped away from assuming my soul's responsibility, I grew more tense and angry with my abuser. As I stepped closer to owning responsibility, I grew angrier with myself. My anger only fed my depression, so either way, I needed to find compassion if I was going to heal. That much I knew for certain from my other healing experiences. The only way out was self-compassion, and self-compassion implied that at some level, I was feeling guilty and/or was blaming someone else entirely. Therefore I deduced, in some way, I must have consented to the circumstances of this life—including sexual abuse.

As an observer of my own life, I noticed that as long as I allowed myself to remain angry and depressed, I continued to draw in abusive circumstances. I chose jobs in which I didn't feel recognized, relationships where I didn't feel respected and honored, and my body continued to challenge me with hormonal imbalance and illness. Whenever my depression lifted a bit, those circumstances began to shift. I figured I had no right to be furious with the person who abused me, if I had simply taken over the job and was abusing myself. Sure, I could continue to blame, but it wasn't going to help me heal. "One abuser at a time," I told myself. "I need to focus on healing the abusive woman inside of me." What became apparent was that if I was committed to lifting the depression, I was going to have to find compassion for myself.

This felt quite foreign to me. It was going take some strong affirmations, deep emotional healing, and some brand new behaviors to re-create myself into a loving compassionate woman toward myself. I read many inspirational books, found a great therapist, nurtured myself with tender massages, spent time in nature, meditated, danced, drew and sang my way to compassion. One way I got to self-compassion was in recognizing that I abused myself because I had been abused. That was a reality I knew intimately well. Another way I accessed greater compassion came when I finally decided to understand why I had chosen this life. Once understood, I could feel love for the wounded little girl inside of me and, eventually I could even feel compassion for the wounded person who abused me. Compassion began with understanding and culminated in love.

As I understood and loved myself for all my shadows and light, forgiveness wasn't even necessary. I was becoming happy and whole, and I eventually loved myself enough to be able to hold that same loving space for my abuser. I came to understand that if I didn't heal, I was likely to continue abusing myself and could therefore do great harm to others around me—out of my misguided woundedness. Once

I recognized the abusive potential in me, I could understand how another person, who was not healed, would continue to act out the abusive reality they knew so well by abusing self and others. My abuser was a person caught in the abuse cycle. This was a person who didn't know how to get out. Like me, maybe this person too accepted they would come into a life of abuse. And maybe hoped they would be able to heal before doing any harm to someone else. And maybe they didn't heal soon enough. I could resent this person for not healing faster, but then I would have to resent myself for not healing faster. Of course, it was all speculation, but they were considerations I could only make as I allowed compassion to become a part of my perspective. What was apparent was that I could no longer assume they were evil.

The only way to end the cycle of abuse was to first experience this newly found love and compassion for myself and then hold that loving, compassionate space for this person to heal. And so I did. I met my abuser and held us in compassion—the kind of compassion that can only come from someone who knows the abusive cycle well, and knows that only compassion redeems us all from it. At first my abuser looked at me as though they couldn't believe what they were hearing. Then, the eyes softened and tears of regret began to fall. As we talked, we found a peaceful place with each other in true love and respect. The wounded little girl in me had finally become a woman and a healer. Now neither of us was an abuser trapped in the cycle. We were two wounded people healing together.

In that moment, love prevailed. Compassion for myself grew into compassion for another. As my compassion deepened over time, the power of my healing gift through sound medicine and my commitment to self-healing became stronger. Our encounter became a reminder to me that the more I healed myself, the more service I could be to others. As I put an end to the abusive tendencies in me, I have energy to help others do the same. As I allowed in greater love for myself, I have greater love and compassion for others. If indeed I did choose a life that included abuse, I must have known I could transform this painful cycle into greater love. At the very least, I was proving to myself I could do it, and that was enough for me to keep on creating more and more love in my world.

BEYOND THE LIMITS OF WOUNDEDNESS

Sometimes it is difficult to know what to do with the hurt and anger you are feeling. There are certainly many excellent therapeutic approaches for addressing these emotions, some of which we have already discussed. I have used many of them from talk therapy with a qualified psychologist to dancing out my emotions on a dance room floor with great success. And yet, there is one method that has helped me release more deep-seated emotional turmoil than any other technique I have used. It might or might not be your best method, but I am compelled to share this with you in case it proves to be as helpful to you as it was and still is for me.

Since this meditation was given to me as a gift to share with others around the world, and I am not aware of it being known by anyone else, I will share it with you here. The meditation was created by Native women of the Northwest and has been asleep for over 100 years, until the time was right for it to be known and practiced again. The time is now. As a woman, you may find this meditation particularly helpful because it works with the sacred energy of a woman's body and spirit. Men have also found it to be helpful; however, keep in mind it is intended to work with women's energy, so if you are a man you will need to connect with your energetic womb and the power of your emotional feelings in order to get the most from this practice. People who have been doing this meditation regularly are discovering issues they have struggled with since they were children, are dissolving easily and in its place, they are finding peace.

It is the only meditation of its type, I am familiar with, that uses human emotion as the doorway to accessing one's greater awakened state of freedom. It has been referred to as a meditation in which one releases the limited body in order to become the limitless self. Because of this description, I fondly refer to it as the Creation Meditation, but even if that spiritual reference doesn't hold meaning for you, I assure you the meditation itself can provide you tremendous relief from emotional pain, along with a deeper relationship with the Divine as you know the sacred nature of the Divine.

This meditation has even proven to be an excellent way to be with your long-held assumptions about life. As we have discussed earlier, assumptions are often based on limited perceptions of truth, and are frequently based in fear that our needs won't be met. Therefore, we usually have strong feelings associated with our assumptions, and these feelings can be taken into the meditation, where they transform into greater truth—the kind of greater truth that sets you free,

There are three steps to the meditation. I strongly recommend you become adept with the first step before progressing to the other two. In the old days, women spent years mastering a single step, so there is no need to rush the process. I'll acquaint you with the first step since it is the one that deals most directly with challenges and the highly charged emotions that come with those feelings of hurt, anger, overwhelm, stuckness and numbness. I suggest you approach the meditation as follows.

Find a quiet moment. Turn off the phone, the TV, the stereo, and commit to not answering the door. This is your time—your sacred time. Tell the children, your spouse, or your roommate to leave you undisturbed for a while. You have sacred work to do. You might want to light a candle, put a vase of flowers nearby, or place a bowl of water near you to set the intention of sacred space, but most of all, what you need most is your solitude.

Begin by breathing gently and sweetly; accepting the nourishment of the air, the day, Spirit, whatever fills you with peace. Then focus on your womb. Allow all your attention to connect to the womb within you. Feel/know/sense/see/hear its darkness—its vastness—its sacred nature, and its ability to hold all possibilities in love and compassion.

Allow your awareness (do not force this, but rather allow) to bring you something you feel limited about. Perhaps it is a fear you have, a concern or doubt, or a feeling that is uncomfortable for you. And hold that limit in the sacredness of your womb. Do not try to fix or change it for that would dishonor the wisdom that lives within the limit. Simply be with the feeling of this limit. As you hold it, feel your compassion swell within you, just as you would feel compassion for a child who was struggling with her or his limits. Simply be in compassion. Do nothing, except BE with it.

Think of it in this way. Your womb and the primordial sacred womb of life are one. Go to your womb and there see/sense the belief that limits you. Hold it, forgive it, and love it within your womb so that it can die a peaceful death. It will, in its own time, transform into a peaceful freedom. It might transform the first time you hold the limit in this way. It might take several or many times, but it will transform—on its own—in the presence of your compassion. You might have a sense of everything inside you opening or relaxing. You might feel more relaxed, happier or freer. Some people see a symbol when they are finished. Some see a beautiful color of light. Others might hear a sound, and still others will know or feel completion. Trust your own intuitive wisdom. This is only an outline, providing plenty of room for your own relationship with the Divine to emerge through the meditation, so give yourself permission to let this meditation truly become your own creative, intuitive experience.

Possibly, at the end you will receive, sense or hear an "I am ...." affirmation that comes deep from within your subconscious. Again, this is not forced. It wells up from the depths of your subconscious to become part of your conscious awareness. These affirmations tend to be particularly effective, because they come from beyond what we think a motivating affirmation should be. From your subconscious mind this affirmation will cause you to feel free and uplifted, even if the word or words do not make sense to your conscious mind. I encourage you to trust what you hear or know the "I am" affirmation to be. Some affirmations of mine include, "I am destiny," "I am sacred," and "I am flight." One woman I know has an I am affirmation that names a country, and though it makes no sense at all, it evokes very powerful feelings of freedom in regard to the limit she held in the meditation. So trust your inner wisdom.

Many people use this meditation to help themselves experience greater self-loving, compassion and the ensuing empowerment and freedom that come from that love. However, if you are finding it difficult to feel compassion, you might visualize yourself as someone else's child in need of love. Or you might need someone to first hold compassionate space for you before you feel able or ready to hold it for yourself. Perhaps some time with a caring healer will help open the door to your own compassion. You may need to simply ask for guidance in your prayers to be led to someone or an awareness that can help you feel your own compassionate spirit. When you have been wounded deeply, this can be very difficult to feel, so be patient and kind with yourself as you open to greater self-love.

FREEING THE NEW YOU INTO BEING

Beyond the hopes and doubts of the healing journey there is knowing—a wisdom that frees us from our fears—a Divine awareness that once found, must become.

Within the human soul there is a longing to become one's full potential, perhaps even more accurately, to recognize each of us as already being what we long to be. We live each day according to what we know in this moment. Yet, often it is what we do not yet know, or remember, that sets us free to experience full and complete healing. That wisdom, and it is ours to discover, lives in the unexplored Divine nature within each of us. We are the agents of our own healing freedom.

PERSONAL ALIGNMENT

A colleague once told me he felt like he was running the parts department at an automotive store. As his friends shared with him their particular challenges, they would describe a part of them wanting one thing, while another part of them wanted another. All the parts were available to them, but his friends weren't sure about which parts they needed to get in place first.

Have you ever felt that way? Part of you wants to have enough time resting to get really healthy. Another part of you would like to be making more money in a meaningful career. Yet another part of you would like to escape to a retreat center where you could sleep most of the day and be cared for the rest of the day. Another part of you would like to have enough energy to solve some problems in the world. And at the moment, none of the parts feel compatible?

This happens to a lot of us during the healing journey. Sometimes what you want and what you need seem to be in conflict. In your journey of discovery, you may feel as though you are being pulled in multiple directions by various desires, both conscious and subconscious. You may become lost or absorbed in the parts. In order to free yourself from the chaos this can create, you need to understand the messages from each of those parts and then invite them into alignment, in one cohesive direction of healing. Your job is to recognize all the seemingly conflicting needs and desires, and decide which is priority, or devise a way in which several needs and wants can be met to varying degrees in your own unique plan. Before you are going to make much progress, your parts need to be in agreement; otherwise, one part of you could wind up sabotaging another part of you.

A friend and coach, who used to be the vice-president of a bank, once told me how she managed her parts. When she could feel the parts of her subconscious and conscious mind fighting for airtime, she would hold a board meeting with herself. She defined the various parts of herself, such as: the Head of Marketing who wanted to see the sales being made and the money coming in; the Head of Community Development who wanted to spend more time enjoying life and creating good-will with others; the Director of Personnel who wanted to take some steps to ensure employee health and wellness, and so on.

She listened carefully to the heads of her internal departments, taking into consideration their range of concerns and desires. Then, as the president of her company, she formed a plan of action that took into account everything she had heard, making sure it was acceptable to all the department heads. Once the plan was formulated and approved, she asked her board for complete support. If necessary, she continued to massage the plan until she could feel total agreement. This clever little theatrical play was her way of ensuring every part of her was in complete alignment. If any part of her had not agreed to her plan of action, she knew there was some likelihood she would undermine her own efforts. Therefore, she found it worth the time and effort to address her own internal debate before taking action.

You may find yourself needing to do something similar in order to ensure no lingering, unaddressed concerns develop into doubts and fears that could sabotage your healing journey. You might even devise your own way of acknowledging your different thoughts and desires. Once you commit fully to complete healing, you are going to need every part of you working in your favor with an approach that reinforces your decision to fully heal.

CLEAR FOCUS AND INTENTION

Like my friend, the former bank vice-president, you need a clear focus and intention for healing in order for it to occur. One of my sound medicine teachers taught me to visualize whatever I was healing in its completely healed state. She emphasized I needed to sustain clear, focused intent if I wanted to see results. I have since discovered if you don't visualize well, feeling or sensing it also works. However, your ability to put all of your energy into that one outcome is paramount.

When I cut myself, while I use sound to close the wounds, I have also learned to visualize the cut being completely sealed as I make the sounds that invite healing. Over time I have developed a confidence in my ability to seal the wound very quickly. (As I described earlier, even a cut normally requiring stitches I have completely healed within a day.) Recently, however, my faith was shaken when I cut my finger with a serrated knife. It left a very jagged wound and the jagged nature of the cut really bothered me. Every time I visualized the wound healing, I first saw that rough blade mangling my finger. That particular cut took twice as long to heal because my mind kept wandering into the past, seeing the serrated blade cutting me. I had to constantly return my focus on seeing it sealed in the present moment.

My emotional response to the nature of the cut was overriding my focus on being healed. Every time I sang to my cut and visualized it being healed, I had to concentrate fully to focus my attention away from the memory of how it happened. I had to remind myself to stay in the present moment where the cut was sealing up. Through this process I was reminded that sometimes staying focused on the present moment—staying focused on the healing—and not the injury or pain takes diligent attention.

FEELING YOURSELF WELL

One of the most challenging aspects to healing is remembering what it feels like to be well so that you can reinforce your healthy reality. Chronic pain, in particular, is a challenge because the pain is fairly constant. And getting to the core issues behind the pain doesn't always cause you to feel better at first. Sometimes it actually feels a bit worse for a little while as you reassemble yourself emotionally. Yet, even with the obstacle of pain, experiencing wellness—even for brief moments—is important in your healing process. Let's say you used a healing approach that gave you relief from your pain for a few minutes. In those minutes you have an experience of your body feeling well. You now have a feeling of wellness you can reinforce.

Feelings motivate us, whether emotional or physical, so your commitment to creating physical wellness every moment you can, sends the body a strong message to be in wellness. You may find it helpful to see a healer, engage in certain exercises or physical therapy, have surgery, meditate, utilize hypnosis, dance, visualize, receive massages, watch comedies, or any number of pain relief approaches. The right approach for you may help you find enough relief from pain long enough to teach your body to become and remain pain-free.

When someone comes to me for a sound medicine session, I know if they are open, there is a good probability they will experience a certain amount of time so immersed in the sounds that the body does not feel any pain or discomfort. For precious minutes their body gets to have a break and experience a state of self-love that allows them to enjoy life. With some help from me or other healers from time to time, and especially with encouragement to use their own healing gifts, they can discover pathways to freeing themselves from pain and reinforcing healthy freedom and wellness.

As I said earlier, I believe everyone has a healing gift inside of them. One of the gifts of the process of healing is uncovering the gift and learning how to use it. Once discovered and used on a regular basis, your gift becomes your tool not only for healing, but also for further spiritual development. This gift is your doorway to the Divine. And there is no better time to access it than when your body and emotions are asking for help, so that you can actually feel the reality of wellness you are creating.

KNOWING IT

Experienced energy healers tend to agree you heal when you *know* you are healing. This is a place of consciousness beyond your will or your feelings. Knowing is a state of awareness beyond intention or intuition. You could describe it as a place where your feelings and will—your intuition and your intention—come together. Developing your intuition and the focus of your will are steps in achieving this state of *knowing*.

When you *know*, you have no remaining doubts. You have considered all of your fears, feelings, intention, motivation, intuition, will and beliefs and they have merged together to become one clear voice of, "I am well." At this point, nothing discourages you, shakes your faith, or detours you from healing. Everything within you is resonating to wellness. Getting to *knowing* is the real journey. Once you *know*, healing occurs rapidly and effectively.

I have noticed a few steps along the way that some of my clients have confused with knowing. The first is the thought form, "I don't want." Knowing that you don't want to be ill or in pain is not the kind of knowing I am talking about here. It is good to know what you don't want, but it is not the crucial belief that will sustain you in your healing. However, defining what pain and discomfort you are ready to be done with can be a great first step in your process.

Getting to what you want is the next step. Finding the words to describe health can be challenging because in my experience our English language seems to have more words for illness and pain, or anti-illness and pain, than it does for health and well-being, so sometimes a little creativity helps. For example, you might decide you want to feel at ease in your body, or you might want to be flexible and limber. Perhaps you would like to describe wellness as vigorous and robust, or wanting your body to feel happy.

The language is important here. Describing your state of wellness in a positive manner is key. Saying, "I am healthy," evokes a stronger positive feeling than stating, "I don't want to be ill." A positive statement is easier for your mind and feelings to translate into an observable outcome. For example, saying, "I want to be cancer-free," is closer to describing what you don't want than describing how you want your body to feel when it is well. Remember feelings motivate, so you need a descriptor that gives you a feeling. Saying, " I want to be done with the fibromyalgia," is a good start. However, describing the energy you will feel in your body when you no longer experience the symptoms is even better. "I want to have abundant energy, flexibility, vigor and joy" would be an even stronger statement and help get you focused on what you are creating. Although this might seem like it must be a state of knowing, it isn't. Indeed, describing the outcome—or affirmations as they are often called—do help us create a state of knowing; however, wanting implies it will happen rather than it is happening now. In a knowing state your affirmations have become reality.

Once you define what you want, the next step is to consciously and full-heartedly choose it. This means you are going to affirm your healing, pray for your healing, act on behalf of your healing, and make positive choices for your healing every day until you feel fully healed. Choosing takes you from naming your desire—"I want" to making a firm commitment supported by action—"I am." If you are working with affirmations, you'll want to reflect this in your statements. For example you might say, "I am feeling healthy and vital." Or, "I am flexible, and I move freely and easily." This is where the healing process really starts taking off. When you choose clearly and consciously, you may be aware of the potential obstacles, yet your clear focus and then your commitment of action carries you through and beyond those challenges.

This is the step in which you might feel tested. For example, you have an opportunity to go out to do something you enjoy when your body is crying for rest. If you are healing physically, you probably don't want to override your body's needs. At the same time, the activity might lift your spirits, so you need to find your best personal balance and this could require some significant honesty about what you need most in any given moment in time. It might also require some creativity. Perhaps flying somewhere to visit friends would lift your spirits, but travel proves to be too taxing on you physically. You could decide to invite your friends over to see you, allowing you to spend precious time with them, while avoiding the stress of travel. Absolute focus and dedication is a must. Let me say that again: absolute focus and dedication is a must if you are serious about healing. Doing what you know is good for your body, mind and spirit some or even most of the time won't cut it. It is going to take as much energy or more to heal as it took for you to become ill, injured or depressed.

When you make your choice, act on that choice with every fiber in your being and all of your conscious awareness. If you decide your body most needs rest in order to heal—rest and don't make excuses as to why you can't rest. If you decide your body needs to cleanse and so you are changing your entire diet—change it. Don't cheat because something tempting is in front of you. If you are following your doctor's advice— follow it. Don't wander in and out of the treatment you have chosen. If it isn't working, certainly consider a new course of action. But if it isn't working because you only partially committed, you are going to have difficulty healing yourself because you aren't putting in as much energy as it took to become ill or injured. Don't let a setback put you in a tailspin. Certainly, you might feel depressed or angry and you need to honor those feelings. Find a safe and effective method for emotional release (personally I like to sound my feelings until they naturally change), rest until you feel peace, and then take stronger, clearer steps on your behalf. There are ups and downs in healing methodologies just like there are in life. Remember to become an astute observer, so that you can determine whether it is your commitment that needs to be strengthened or a methodology that needs to change.

"I know" follows your commitment of action. As you act on behalf of your own healing, over and over again, your confidence increases if you allow it. You are beyond seeing the potential. Now you are taking action in your healing with great diligence because you know deep down in your cells that something wonderful is taking place. When you know you are healing, you are. When I sing to a cut finger, I don't wonder *if* it is going to heal quickly, I know it is and it does. When I sing to someone, I don't wonder *if* my sounds are going to help, I know they help. *If* reflects doubt and doubt affects healing progress. In fact, doubt is one of the greatest inhibitors to healing. So if doubt comes up, go back a step to focusing and acting on your own behalf until you know.

The healing journey is one of empowerment, where you claim your birthright to heal yourself. Throughout that journey, doubts are going to come up to be considered, understood, and loved with compassion. Then you get to transform doubts into positive energy in your healing.

You get to access the Divine within you, creating from the depth of your *knowing*.

My dear friend, Julie, shared with me a significant healing experience she recently had with a breast tumor. Though she was receiving skilled medical help, she has a tremendous healing gift and a great capacity for *knowing* when healing is occurring. It was her state of *knowing* that she believes made the biggest difference in complete healing and in communicating with medical staff.

Following a mammogram, her doctor informed Julie she had an atypical ductal hyperplasia (ADH), so her doctor recommended she see a surgeon. She decided to research this condition before seeing the surgeon and discovered several interesting facts. She learned ADH tumors are typically benign, but indicate the likelihood of cancer. People with ADH are four out of five times more likely to get breast cancer. In the United States removal is recommended; however, in England, Australia and Canada, for example, doctors observe and monitor them until there is an indication the spot is cancerous.

Her surgeon did indeed recommend surgery. Julie explained to him she understood the risks he had outlined for her, but told the surgeon she was not going to have surgery immediately, preferring to have another biopsy in six months to see if the situation had changed and if surgery was indicated. The surgeon agreed there was no urgency at this point for a lumpectomy. They agreed on another biopsy in six months.

During the six months, Julie utilized several natural healing modalities with which she had experienced healing successes in the past. She told me as the time for the second biopsy was nearing that she was quite certain the tumor was benign and either completely gone or nearly gone. Her regular doctor ordered the second biopsy and the radiology department declined to do it because a lumpectomy was the only medically approved procedure proper in this case that met the "medical standard of care."

She understood the department's concern that if in the future it did become cancerous she might decide to sue them because they had not followed the proper standard of medical care, but she took responsibility for her own decision. She knew her body and knew she didn't have cancer. She knew she was healing it with energy medicine.

She knew it with absolute certainty. She wanted the hospital to do the second biopsy to show with their diagnostic equipment that the tumor had been either reduced or was gone because of the alternative medicine she had been using.

She wrote a very professional and rational letter to the president of the hospital, with a copy to the head of radiology, her doctor and the surgeon telling them she understood their concerns. She wanted the biopsy to demonstrate that the lump was gone. She had chosen to use alternative methods and did not want to use their "standard of medical care," understood the issue of liability and would sign any waiver of liability relieving them from all responsibility if she later developed cancer because she postponed obtaining a lumpectomy at this time. Being an attorney, she understood the legal ramifications and was able to address them to the satisfaction of the hospital and head of radiology.

In return, she received a reasonable and polite response from the president of the hospital stating that a doctor in the radiology department agreed to do a second biopsy. She made her appointment and during the second biopsy, the radiologist had difficulty finding the lump. The new mammogram showed it had been reduced over 50%. The radiologist doing the biopsy told her, "I don't know what you are doing, but keep it up. It is working." He removed the remaining small portion of the lump during the biopsy, and notified her doctor that the remaining portion was benign with no indication of cancer.

When she arrived for the second appointment, she told me the radiologist initially spoke to her as if she was being a difficult or recalcitrant child, when she was clearly conscious about what she was choosing. When he finally found the lump and realized how much it had reduced in size his voice and entire manner changed. He then spoke to her respectfully like an intelligent adult. His initial condescending demeanor could have caused her to begin doubting herself and her own healing abilities, but Julie did not falter in the presence of his skepticism. She was strong enough in her own knowing that she recognized his cynicism as his own. His opinion did not affect her inner knowing.

I asked Julie to describe what it meant to *know* it was healed. How was that different from *thinking* it was healed, I wondered?

Here is how she responded: "If I had been feeling any fear, then the fear would indicate doubt and that would mean I had something I needed to look at very carefully. If I had been in denial, I wouldn't have been really looking at it and being with it objectively in my healing meditations. Knowing meant I was looking right at the problem and I was experiencing no fear. If I hadn't known for certain I could heal it, I would have gotten the recommended treatment."

Julie has had some excellent medical support and physicians caring for her throughout many years. She has followed the advice of her doctors with great confidence, so to be so sure that the course of treatment was inappropriate and to say "No," was contrary to her usual relationship with doctors. It took a lot of courage to say, "No," to surgery. She told me she couldn't have done this 10 years ago, but at this time in her life she felt she had to be true to herself. She could only do this because she absolutely knew without any doubt that she was choosing the best course of action for herself. She admits if she had experienced any doubt at all, following the recommended procedures would have been wise. She only proceeded with her course of action because she *knew*.

SUSTAINING THE ENERGY

My sound medicine teacher taught me the importance of sustaining the healing vibration I created. You might remember, she encouraged me to sing, see, and feel the healing I was creating for an uninterrupted, clearly focused 10 seconds. When I began I was amazed at how quickly my mind wandered away from my focus. As soon as my focus was in place, my mind drifted off to something else, seemingly more interesting. Then when I was holding my focus for several seconds, I noticed I became bored unless the feeling and energy behind my focus was quite high. In other words, intensity of both focus and feeling were important for healing to occur.

Many of us give up too soon because we have not yet learned how to sustain intensity of focus and feeling. Because this can feel like hard work, I do my best to make it fun. Celebrating every little success helps, and so does inviting my friends and family to celebrate with me. I find positive ways to acknowledge my healing accomplishments so that I don't inadvertently undo my healing while I'm celebrating. In other words, if I'm eating a specialized diet to help me heal, I don't eat something off my diet to celebrate. However, I might suggest a toast to my improving health with a drink that is on my diet.

When I feel my energy starting to slide, sometimes I call a friend and ask him or her to help me get through my slump to a place where I feel more positive and encouraged about my healing journey. It is amazing how often I have been too focused on what is not healing yet, instead of noticing how far I have come. Friends are great for helping me get a reality check and supporting me with their confidence in me. They can also help me get to a place where I am laughing at my own seriousness, which shifts my energy to a positive place instantly.

Engaging your creativity can make a big difference in sustaining energy. Remember, creativity can help you get your mind off your discomfort, help you uncover core issues behind your illness, and even help you sustain yourself in your process of becoming well. It is fairly well known that listening to music while exercising helps you exercise longer. Have you noticed how listening to a book on tape makes a long drive seem shorter? You can use your creative talents to help sustain your moments of feeling well for longer periods of time, even with joy and enthusiasm.

THE POWER OF PRAYER

I absolutely believe in the power of prayer and affirmations to change and sustain energy. Well-considered, positive affirmations and prayers can boost your energy in moments. When you create your healing prayers, consider carefully the words you are choosing and the intentions behind them. Additionally I recommend becoming clear about the prayers you are willing to accept into your energetic field. It may be difficult to believe, but prayers can actually limit your healing progress as much as they can help.

This lesson really came home for me when I was doing a sound healing session for a friend. One of the benefits of working with sound is that my capacity to hear on the inner planes of reality has increased. Intuitively, I sometimes pick up beliefs and thoughts that are interfering with the healing. As I was offering healing sounds I heard prayers that others had said for her that were actually causing her greater discomfort.

My friend is a very spiritual woman with a faith in Spirit that is profoundly inspiring. However, she did not hold the same religious beliefs as some of her family. Their prayers were suggesting she find her faith in Jesus through her healing, and that she be granted her healing as she found him. Those prayers, for all their good intention, were at the essence affirming she stay in pain until she agreed to a path of faith acceptable to her family. Since these prayers weren't compatible with her own spiritual beliefs, and she was graciously receiving the prayers of her family, the conflicting thought forms were creating distress that only contributed to her illness.

Putting conditions on our prayers for others can actually be a harmful way to pray when it comes to healing. In reference to this example it could be helpful to remember that there is no published record of Jesus putting the condition of converting to Judaism on anyone who asked for healing. We would do well to follow his example when it comes to our prayers for others. Healing does not need to be attached to a specific religion in order to occur. There are great healers in all spiritual traditions. It is our birthright, not something we need to bargain for. Bargaining limits the way in which the Divine can work on our behalf.

I suggested my friend create a strong clear intention and prayer for her own healing, and affirm that any and all prayer said on her behalf be accepted if they were in alignment with her own intention and highest good. Once she clarified her intention, her healing accelerated. Since then I have suggested to clients they share with their loved ones exactly what they are praying for so it is easy for others to align with their prayerful intentions.

Another reason to carefully consider how we frame a prayer is to consider the energy limits you may be creating through a prayer. For example, many of us learned to ask when we pray. There is nothing wrong with asking, but if you are serious about creating wellness, asking may be a weaker form of prayer for you. Asking suggests that you might get a "yes" or "no" for an answer. We ask when we are little children, so asking comes for many of us with all of the hopes and fears of maybe or maybe not getting what we asked for. It's the energy of *fear* that we might not get what we asked for that makes this form of prayer less effective for many of us.

If you are going to ask, ask with complete certainty that the Divine inspiration behind your request simply must be positively acknowledged, provided it is good for everyone involved. If you think you might have a shred of fear or doubt in your request, you may find the answer to your prayer reflects your fear. In that case, you are better off affirming what you are creating in your healing, positively and decisively, knowing the desire comes from Divine within you. As your intended reality unfolds over time, you sustain your faith and belief by nourishing your prayer daily with your love and encouragement.

One of my great teachers about asking was a five-year-old girl. We had just finished an event I facilitated and everyone was enjoying a great potluck of wonderful dishes they had brought. We hadn't gotten to the dessert items yet, though a perky little five year old was eyeing a delicious looking chocolate cake. She asked her mother if she could have a piece and her mother told her she would need to ask me. A bright-eyed and excited little five year old turned around to look at me and asked with all the enthusiasm exuding from her little body, "Misa, can I have a piece of cake?"

I was completely compelled by the excitement and confidence in her voice. Inside I was praying she wasn't a diabetic because it would have broken my heart to say, "No." In a second, I decided her mother would have directed her to a better choice if that had been the case, and answered her with a big grin, saying simply, "Yeah, you can have a piece of cake."

This little gal couldn't contain her excitement any longer. She threw her arms around me, grinning back with a big, "Thank you, Misa!"

Watching her savor every bite of her chocolate cake, I wondered what my own life would be like if I asked with that kind of confidence and eagerness, thanked with such genuine gratitude and gusto, and surrendered to the sheer delight and enjoyment of the gifts I had been given.

GRATITUDE

One of the most effective forms of prayer is gratitude. I have a friend who has made this the only form of prayer he uses. Listening to him pray makes me feel good. When he finishes his prayers, I feel absolutely confident he is going to create what he has prayed for. Here is how he does it. He begins with prayers of thanks for what he has already received and what he is already experiencing. And he says these prayers with heart. They aren't just rote words. Then he gives thanks for what he desires, saying it as though it has already happened. He might say something like, "Thank you for our new house with a view." "Thank you for sending new and inspiring people to serve." "Thank you for my excellent health and good energy."

In each of these examples, he would have been house shopping, looking for new clients, or healing from a virus. I heard this house prayer on more than one occasion. He looked at a lot of houses and rejected most of them because they didn't fit the picture he had in his mind. He had an image of what he wanted, he had already given thanks for it, and now he needed to keep looking until he found it. He did find his house and you should see it—it's absolutely gorgeous.

I have even heard him offer these prayers spontaneously. He will be outside and suddenly say, "Thank you, Spirit, for such a beautiful day." Then he breathes in the sunshine and fresh air. Or after house looking, he would spontaneously say, "Thank you, Spirit. Each house is closer to what I want." If he is confused, letdown or struggling with something, I have heard him say, "Thank you, Spirit, for providing me with guidance."

How often in your own healing journey have you felt confused, disappointed or hopeless? How would your energy shift simply by offering a heartfelt prayer of gratitude? "Thank you for providing me with guidance so I can make a good decision." "Thank you for filling me with renewed hope." "Thank you for all of the ways, Divine One, you have been helping me in seen and unseen ways." How would the experience of your healing journey change with a simple, heart-inspired prayer of gratitude?

Prayers of confidence and enthusiasm, and prayers of gratitude can fill you with awe. You can feel the Divine flowing within you as you acknowledge all the ways you are already being taken care of, looked after, loved, encouraged, informed, inspired, healed, helped or touched. Sometimes you feel completely alone when you are on this journey. And in some ways you are because ultimately this is a journey between you and the Divine. Yet, there are so many ways in which beautiful and miraculous awareness and relationships are opening up—some going on in the background that haven't emerged fully into view. Acknowledging these priceless gifts can give you a whole new perspective as to what your healing journey is really all about.

GO AS DEEP INTO YOUR SUBCONSCIOUS AS YOU CAN

Yet another consideration with prayer is to hold the clarity of your prayerful intent deep within your subconscious. The deeper your intentions are within your subconscious, the more significant and lasting your healing transformation will be. Stating your prayers before you dream at night, meditating on your prayers and listening to guidance from the Divine, hypno-therapy, and trance or journey work, for example, all help you access and understand your core fears and transform them with your intentions at a very profound level. This is one way you can get all of your "parts" working together toward your Divine intention.

At one point in my life, abandonment issues were coming up repeatedly with my partner. I became quite irritable and anxious just before he left on trips. After too many fights centered around my irritability, I decided to do something about this. Like I usually do, I meditated for guidance about how to best approach healing my anxiety. My meditation showed me I came into the world with a predisposition to feel abandoned. In reflecting on my meditation, I decided my best point of transformation was in the womb, and I knew I wanted help getting there. My intuition led me to a healer I had met years before. She had recently learned a healing technique that we both expected would help me journey into my mother's womb before I was born.

There, lying quietly on her massage table, beneath her healing hands, I journeyed until I was looking at my fetus, nearly ready to be born. I heard my subconscious mind say to my tiny self, "You know that abandonment thing we do in life?

"Yes," my tiny self replied.

"Let's not do it, okay?" I asked.

"Okay," she said.

I could then feel the cells of my body changing as I adopted and integrated this new belief. Since then, I have not felt that intense irritability or anxiety when my beloved is preparing to leave. I might miss him while he is gone, but I'm not anxious and cranky before he leaves. It seems to me because I was deep in my inner world, trusted the assistance of a skilled practitioner, and because I was truly ready for complete transformation, my subconscious mind responded immediately and fully. The depth of the process allowed me to fundamentally change.

Even if you are not ready to do trance work of this nature yet, being able to visualize in a profoundly relaxed state can be very effective in healing. I once had a client in her mid-seventies whose heart needed to be strengthened before she considered surgery for an aneurism. I spent several days with her, helping her create a healthier heart for herself. She had particularly strong visualizations, so in a guided visualization I suggested she let her subconscious mind give her a symbol for strengthening her heart. Immediately, she saw a pool of water and so her pool became her focal point as she held the intention of a strong heart. It is significant to note she simply observed the water while holding her intention. She wasn't consciously doing anything to the water, but as she observed, the water changed as she held her intention. I supported her with sound medicine, but the clarity of intention was hers. About a week later her daughter called with results from a recent set of x-rays. My client had grown a brand new valve to her heart.

SOMETIMES HEALING COMES IN STEPS

In my first career as a Special Education teacher, I learned to take any goal and break it down into a series of tiny steps that would ensure success as the student moved toward developing a new skill. I have noticed, when it comes to healing, that as adults we often expect ourselves to meet our goals practically the minute we create them. Anything short of immediate and miraculous results and we think we have failed. Noticing the progressive steps we are taking can help us sustain our energy, recognize our real success and feel good about our improvements.

Let's say you are changing a negative belief that is contributing to an illness. You have accurately identified the belief, now it is time to replace it with a new, healthier one. In this case, perhaps you have contracted a cold virus. Since you aren't aware of a medical cure for the cold virus, your thought about the matter might sound like this, "There is no cure, so I just need to ride it out." However, if you decide to open your consciousness to healing, you might decide to affirm, "I am healing quickly and effectively." Your mind and body are totally committed to a new response, as you change from the old thought to a new belief. Here is a typical series of progressive steps in your awareness as you adopt the belief of your new affirmation:

1. First—you catch yourself after the old thought that there is nothing you can do, and immediately affirm your new belief. This happens several times and then…

2. Second—you catch yourself as you are thinking the old belief and immediately affirm your new belief. You do this a number of times and then….

3. You catch yourself just before you think the old belief and immediately affirm your new belief. You do this a few times and then….

4. Finally—the old belief doesn't even come to mind. The new belief now becomes your new response.

You may contract a cold virus several times before your new belief kicks in fully and you are healing as soon as you notice you have contracted the virus. Your next step might then be to look for a way to address the virus without waiting to become sick. Your progress may be slower than you would like, but if you stay with your intention, you will eventually create a whole new belief system, and an entirely new way to respond and prevent illness. You might create a whole new affirmation, such as, "I remain completely healthy all year long." By the way, if this example sounds far-fetched to you, I have met more than one person who has not experienced a cold in years, each with their own story about how they prevent themselves from catching colds.

Healing is less effective if I get in a big hurry to get out of my discomfort and attempt to force it, and end up rushing the natural steps or progression. Let's say I am taking healing herbs to address an allergic reaction. My naturopath has told me what to take and how much to take, but I decide twice as much of a healing herb means I'll heal twice as fast. The result of my increased dosage is yet more discomfort and new symptoms. Rushing the healing process along is not necessarily an effective way to heal.

Of course, we sometimes need to utilize an aggressive treatment in order to turn a very serious illness around quickly. Life-threatening illnesses and injuries may require an immediate, assertive response. Yet, there are many cases where we can heal ourselves at a gentle pace compatible with steady physical progress over time. Some years ago, I was lying in bed in intense discomfort. I hurt so badly, I could hardly lift my head. I can sing medicine songs in my head and have them work effectively for me, but I couldn't even raise enough energy to hear the song I needed. I humbly asked the Divine for some guidance. I was not willing to lie in bed and suffer, and I was convinced there was something I could do for myself, if only I could discover it.

After asking for help, I became very quiet inside, observing my thoughts. I was compelled to breathe with an awareness of my breath soothing every cell. I visualized my breath as a soft feather, very gently caressing the edges of my pain, brushing away discomfort and replacing distress with ease. It took me a while to use this "feather breath" on my entire body, and I was amazed at how well I was able to maintain my focus until my entire body had been soothed in the breath. When I finished I promptly fell into a peaceful sleep. I awoke some time later with enough energy to sing a healing song to myself, which again resulted in me being sleepy. By the time I awoke again, I had enough energy and mental clarity to identify the source of my pain and complete the healing process.

With the grace of Divine inspiration, I met the illness where I was able to respond effectively. Over time, my stamina grew and I was able to increase the potency and frequency of my response because I was able to sing as much as I felt the need for it, with enough energy to keep my attention firmly fixed on my healing. I even developed enough strength to finally get help. The entire process invited and welcomed healing to occur. I was too weak to get out of bed to get help, and I could have attempted to force myself to sing when I was so very ill, but the feather breath was so much more accessible to me. It was easier, gentler and effective given my physical condition. Healing was clearly a process, taking place one step at a time.

I have needed to spend a fair amount of time keeping my body healthy. A friend once told me I have a body like a sports car. When it goes it really goes, but it seems to need to spend a lot of time in the shop. I now know I am my healthiest when I do a lot of preventative maintenance, focusing on increasing my vitality and health, rather than waiting until I break down and then need to get myself well. Because I have learned to take better care of my body and emotions, these days my physical and emotional challenges are minimal. However, because I used to spend a fair amount of time "in the shop," I know how difficult it was to accomplish life goals and dreams when I wasn't feeling well. Yet attempting to rush my healing process never worked. My healing was simply part of my spiritual journey and I eventually learned to honor that.

Honoring my journey meant creating fewer expectations of myself. There were times it was better for me to take a job where I could enjoy helping people with my talents without the pressures of owning a company. There were times I chose to keep my material needs down to a minimum so I could devote more time and energy to healing. There were other times I chose to be self-employed because I could manage my own time, allowing enough opportunity for meditation and energy healing that seemed to be making the biggest difference for me. Healing became my primary job. Sometimes I was more conscious of that than others, but as I reflect, healing was often the focus, and needed to be the focus, of my attention.

Now that my body is strong and I am at peace with myself emotionally, I find my life work to be exhilarating and stimulating. My life force is bubbling over with plenty to share with others without becoming depleted. There have been so many times I have tried to push my life work into the world. I was so anxious to fulfill my soul purpose, but pushing only caused me to become ill, yet again. Allowing myself to heal, allowing my work to blossom naturally, and allowing myself to find the natural rhythm of steps that works for me have carried me into the essence of the Divine flowing inside of me.

AHHHH....SURRENDER

Have you noticed in your own healing journey that sometimes you are devoting a lot of your life force trying to get control of your healing? It doesn't work very well does it? You don't make your body heal. Healing simply isn't something to be controlled, though it can be invited, and you can surrender yourself to healing. Surrender is about giving up the fight. Fighting to be well isn't effective because fighting causes you to tense up. Remember, you don't heal as well when you are tense as you do when you are relaxed. So if you are fighting for health, what you really need to do is surrender.

You don't want to surrender in defeat. That's not the kind of surrendering I'm talking about. This act of surrender is about surrendering fully and completely to your absolute health. You can surrender to vigor, vitality, happiness, comfort, flexibility, ease in your body or any other positive feeling outcome of wellness. You can even surrender fully to the Divine. When you surrender in this manner, your body relaxes. You might even describe it as sinking in, or giving in, to feeling good. Remember my friend the healing writer who in her process surrenders to joy? Isn't that a lovely way to invoke healing? If you haven't tried surrendering in your healing process, give it a whirl. You might discover a whole new way of inviting yourself to heal.

BE SEDUCTIVE—WELCOME HEALING IN

More often than not, I have discovered I make the most healing progress when I *welcome* healing into my mind, body and spirit. This is a subtle concept, but an important one. Remember we discussed that you probably won't get very far with using only your will. Our consciousness likes to be coaxed, encouraged and supported. Think about it this way: if you are spending time with someone new who has a romantic interest in you, what is going to better communicate their loving regard for you—gentle and kind caresses or being pushed forcefully? If your new love is trying to will or force you to do something with them, he or she probably isn't communicating love to you. On the other hand, if they sensitively offer you an invitation to join them in a great adventure together, you might interpret that as more caring or loving. Your subconscious mind knows the difference, whether you are considering romance or healing. You probably won't be able to force your subconscious to heal, but you can seductively invite it into the grand adventure of your health and well-being.

What I love about energetic healing is that if it is done properly, it can be a very gentle, noninvasive approach—especially if healing is welcomed and not forced. Energetic healing can actually feel pleasant, free you from discomfort, and reveal insights about addressing the illness, injury or depression at its core. The subconscious and conscious minds are invited to fully engage in your well-being. Your healing time becomes a respite from your usual activities and keeps you mindful about your commitment to health. Most of all, the freedom you experience after an energetic healing session is absolutely luscious. ·

FREEING THE DIVINE WITHIN

Healing is a journey of freedom. You get to imagine how you would like to experience life and then free yourself to become what you imagine. To heal is to know the power of the Divine within you. Even if your journey takes you to crossing to the other side sooner than you might have expected, the crossing sets you free to a greater realization of yourself in the arms of the Divine. The healing journey in both life and death is a sacred opportunity to awaken fully to your Divine essence.

Discovering the Divine spark within you and igniting it is the whole point of the healing journey, and once ignited the need to suffer disappears. Any suffering that might need to ever have been done has been done, so you are free to live as blessed, healthy, beautiful beings of Divine fulfillment, purpose and service to others. When you no longer need to focus your life force energy on healing, just imagine the energy you will have to devote to your special and unique purpose of existence.

My sincerest desire is that every person on this planet discovers their essential self through their healing processes. While you are created, you are also a creator. It is your Divine birthright to uncover and explore that essence within. There is a place within you that knows your perfection as a Divine being. Healing is a vehicle through which you have an opportunity to awaken to your Divine essence—your limitless and perfect nature—unencumbered by suffering and completely free.

Imagine sealing cuts, healing bruises and repairing damaged muscles with your thoughts. Imagine attending to your body and emotions so well, you rarely became upset, ill or injured. Imagine a world in which you grew your own new organ or repaired it when one of them failed to work properly anymore. Imagine healing yourself and helping to heal others in love, kindness and gentleness. Imagine, when the day comes, simply leaving your body and crossing to the other side without illness or pain. Imagine the Divine flowing through you, filling you with bliss as a part of everyday life. This is the world I am dreaming into existence.

This might sound far-fetched to you, but I have seen enough of these possibilities in real life that I'm willing to hold this vision in my thoughts and prayers until we as humans achieve the seemingly impossible. Our parents, and especially our grandparents or great grandparents could probably not have imagined how much information we learn and manage today. Look at the technological creations of the 20th century—cars, planes, telephones, computers, electric lights and cinema—so many remarkable inventions in so little time. And all of it came from our inspiration and intelligence. What are we capable of doing that we have not even imagined yet? One of our greatest gifts is free will—our right to choose how we will experience our lives. I wonder, how limitless might that free will be?

About the Author

Reverend Misa Hopkins is a metaphysical teacher and speaker. Co-founder and spiritual director of the New Dream Foundation, committed to creating global spiritual family, she is dedicated to serving the needs of people seeking greater healing, peace and purpose in their lives. As a former special education teacher and organizational development facilitator, and now as a spiritual counselor and healer, she is an astute observer of motivation and human potential. After spending several years studying with Cherokee medicine women, Reverend Misa now helps people around the world discover their own natural abilities to heal, and to embrace their unique mystical and Divine gifts.

For more information about Misa Hopkins' The Root of All Healing Workbook, healing CDs, workshops and services, please visit http://www.misahopkins.com.

LaVergne, TN USA
25 November 2009
165225LV00004B/24/P